CAMOUFLAGED SHAME (UNCENSORED)

A Path to Redemption After Military Sexual Trauma

JJ PIZARRO-HARPE

JJP -Harpe LLC

CAMOUFLAGED SHAME
(UNCENSORED)

Contents

Dedication

I dedicate this book to my fellow women veterans, especially those who have experienced and camouflaged the shame of military sexual trauma (MST) but continue to fight the battle in their heads every day while manipulating the world around them. I pray they find peace, joy, and love so they will thrive in ways they never imagined. May they find their path to healing and learn to love themselves again.

This book is dedicated also to those who could not fight any longer and lost their lives because of the pain they could not bear. To all the families left behind with no understanding of their struggles, I pray you find peace. My ultimate wish is for anyone who has been affected by the nightmare of MST to find healing.

To my three beautiful daughters, Brionna, Demetria and Erica, may you always know that you never have to struggle alone regardless of what it may be. I am here for you without judgement or conditions. I pray that you never have to endure the pain I had to. Please listen to your gut, and don't second-guess your feelings if you sense something or someone is not right. May you all find your true calling in love, life, and careers without having to battle the nightmares I did.

To my handsome sons, Darren and Devon, remember all our private talks. I will always be your soft place when you need me and your tough love when you deserve it. We have been through so much together, and I am so thankful for the love you taught me to receive and give without boundaries. You too have lived through my hell, and you saw the ugly face of post-traumatic stress disorder in me. My pain was not yours to carry, and I pray you also find healing and forgiveness for my failure to do better in those moments.

To all my children, learn to live your life to the fullest. Manifest your true potential so you can live your best lives. Learn to love without boundaries. Be your authentic selves and learn to love yourselves first so you can love others the way you deserve to be loved. Learn to laugh at your mistakes and be okay with them while you grow from those mistakes. Most important, remember to keep God as the center of your life and you will always have the guidance you need. The sky is the limit.

To my husband Darius, my best friend and soulmate, you are my blessing. All the pain I battled and wrestled with before you came back into my life was worth it now that I am your wife. I feel so blessed to have been given the opportunity to be your wife and spend the rest of my life with you. I dedicate this book to you for all the unconditional support you have always given and continue to give me. Even when we were just friends back on Marine Corps Air Station Kaneohe Bay Hawaii, you were always selflessly there for me as my true friend. You know my deepest, darkest moments and yet you continue to love me. You make me feel safe, loved, heard, and valued. Without your love and support, I would never have had the strength to write and finish and publish this book.

Acknowledgments

I thank my heavenly Father for His grace, mercy, and favor. Without Him, I would never have made it through these years. My faith has provided me with the comfort I needed when I didn't find it in the world.

I also thank those who doubted me and told me I would be nothing. Their doubts gave me the motivation to push through and use my inner strength to overcome all the obstacles in my path.

Thank you to my amazing children Darren, Devon, Brionna, Demetria and Erica for being my ultimate inspiration. I am blessed to be your mother; I have no doubt God planned things with you all for a reason. You each have taught me to be a better mother and inspired me to seek how I can be better person every day. I am so proud of what you have become so far, and I can't wait to share in all of your successes and blessings in the future.

Thank you to my most incredible husband, Darius, without whom I wouldn't be where I am today. God brought you back into my life when I was ready to receive all you had to give. I am so very grateful for the wonderful man, father, brother, and husband you are. Your unconditional love, support, loyalty, protection, and compassion will never be taken for granted.

Thank you, Dr. Jimenez. You gave me the tools to blossom into the woman I am today. I am so blessed to have you as my guide and clarity. You taught me to challenge my beliefs and see alternative realities. I will forever appreciate everything you taught me. Thank you for calling me out when I needed it and for reminding me who I really am. I will use my toolbox and smile, because you showed me that I had the tools, I just needed to open the box and start using them.

I thank my father, who instilled in me the ability to push myself no matter how hard that could be. He taught me that a man should provide and protect, not take away from and hurt you. Thank you for also teaching me how important family is.

Thank you to my mother for reminding me that I can be loved. When I needed encouragement, she gave it. She made sure to remind me of all the goodness in me regardless of what others had to say.

Thank you to my bonus mother. She inspired me to be the best mother I could be. Watching her sacrifices and her strength through adversity, reminded me that I could do it all if I put my mind to it.

Thank you to my favorite titi Patricia. You taught me how to be giving and love others even when they don't deserve it. She was always available to me with her doors and arms wide open whenever I needed her. I will always appreciate the laughter and special memories we have shares throughout the years.

Thank you to everyone who has supported me along the way all these years. May the Lord bless you and provide you with strength and knowledge you need to conquer all your dreams as I am trying to do.

I want to especially give a special thanks to the following individuals for their support and inspiration this past year. This book was written for many, but each of them gave me encouragement and believed in what I had to say so it could come to fruition.

Abena Weber
Adam Issa
Adrienne Goldsworthy
Antonio Souchet
Arlene Taylor
Autumn Austin
Chandra Heard
Daisy Lee Montalvo
Denise Hendrickson
Donna Brookes
Isabel Soltero
Jessika Pizarro
Johnnie Jackson
Kedrick Young
Kimberly Roland
Kristina Romero
Linda Leonard
Linda Lewis-James
Christina Thomas
Louis Molina
Lourdes Mendoza
Luzinda Pizarro
Mariam Saba
Mayling Pizarro-Acevado
Michelle Schriock
Molly Sweat
Natasha Rosario-Wylie
Reginald Jhons
Ricardo Ellison
Rolando Seda
Sandra Del Signore
Sarah Pizarro
Stacey Benson
Tamiko Ralston

TiOcea Hagins
Torrell, Jackson
Trinidad Hernandez
Wanda Hernandez
Yolanda Cullins
Zenina Malden

CAMOUFLAGED SHAME

(UNCENSORED)
A Path to Redemption after Military Sexual Trauma

JJ PIZARRO-HARPE

YOUNG JEANETTE

Military Sexual Trauma

Military sexual trauma (MST) is the term that the Department of Veterans Affairs uses to refer to sexual assault or repeated, threatening sexual harassment that occurred while the Veteran was in the military. It includes any sexual activity where someone is involved against his or her will—he or she may have been pressured into sexual activities (for example, with threats of negative consequences for refusing to be sexually cooperative or with implied faster promotions or better treatment in exchange for sex), may have been unable to consent to sexual activities (for example, when intoxicated), or may have been physically forced into sexual activities. Other experiences that fall into the category of MST include unwanted sexual touching or grabbing; threatening, offensive remarks about a person's body or sexual activities; and/or threatening or unwelcome sexual advances. —US Department of Veterans Affairs

PROLOGUE

If you are reading this book because you to have experienced traumas similar to mine, please be aware this book is not meant to be the solution to overcome the trauma you've endured but more as a facilitator and/or an inspiration for you to seek the help in healing your own spirit. I pray this book can show you that there are different paths to healing for everyone, but the paths are there for you to discover. Each of us needs to find the path right for ourselves. There are many treatments and routes to healing, my hope is that you discover the path that works best for you.

For family members looking to understand and support their loved ones, when you read this book, be open to seeing things from our perspective. You cannot heal us. Please be patient and kind. Judgment and harsh criticism should never be your approach. Some days, you might need only to listen. For me, encouragement and support were the best medicine most of the time. Don't take it personally when she or he wants space and keeps to himself or herself. We need time to process sometimes because trauma caused by sexual assault is difficult to process.

* * *

This book is about my experiences while serving in the US Marine Corps when I suffered military sexual trauma and harassment. I also touch on some of the experiences from growing up of which I be-lieve contributed to my being susceptible to this abuse. For so long, I allowed my shame and the fear, that no one would believe me, to guide my decisions. I thought I needed to seek justice to find peace, but I got justice, validation, and peace by forgiving myself and being blessed to have special people who sometimes unknowingly led me step by step down my path to recovery and healing.

* * *

In no way am I blaming the US Marine Corps, as a matter of fact, I blame the small group of individuals that use laws within in order to protect themselves. I am, and always will be proud of the service I gave to my country. Unfortunately, these same people can be found everywhere.

* * *

Growing up in the Bronx during the '80s and early '90s was rough. My parents were very protective of me, and I grew up very sheltered. My parents separated and divorced when I was about three. Though not the norm in the '70s, my father was granted full custody of me. Since my parents were divorced, I occasionally visited my mother on weekends – well when she decided to pick me up - and lived with my dad and stepmother full time during the week.

I was a sad little girl. Unbeknown to my father, I yearned to be with my mother mostly because I felt the disdain certain family members demonstrated toward me where I lived full time. I endured some questionable treatment, physical and mental abuse, disparagement, and belittlement at the hands of this individual but was too afraid to tell anyone since I was threatened with more harm if I told.

My mother had no idea that she made me feel unwanted. I never told her as a child for fear that she may reject me or not come around even more. It is very hard when you have a parent who is given visitation allowances, but they do not actively demonstrate consistency with that grant. It made me feel unloved because even though they were granted visitation on the weekends, she frequently didn't show up, so I didn't get to see her as often as I desired. Frequently, I wondered if she even wanted me around. It was as if I was more of a burden than a child that was wanted and loved. At times, it felt like months would pass before she would come to see me. As a child, I had no way of conveying what I felt other than internally just feeling ignored and unloved. The sadness and despair slowly grew inside. I would daydream about being with her believing that then I would be loved. Because of this, I yearned to be with her even more. I had rather be with the person who at least paid some attention to me than be with the people who barely noticed me unless it was to chastise or demean me in some way like at my fathers house.

It was a different time in the '70s. Seriously, I grew up in an era when children were seen, not heard, so my words fell on deaf ears. According to most adults, children didn't know anything let alone how to articulate how they felt, so they were brushed aside. My feelings were not validated in any way, and no one cared to try. I can't imagine how no one noticed the sadness in me.

Sadly, my family also kept secrets. I was taught early on how to keep family secrets. If I saw something, I was expected to keep quiet about it. If someone did something to me and I told, I was threatened with harm if I ever spoke about it again. Perhaps it was not their intention, but that fostered trust issues in me. Whom could I trust? I am just grateful that it wasn't worse than it was. I was manipulated into keeping secrets for adults then put in the position to choose in my young mind how to deal with the information. I was given the responsibility of having potentially damaging info then having to know how to withhold it without telling anyone else the truth.

* * *

I once was a happy, fearless little girl who believed in fairy tales and happy endings. But it wasn't long before something changed deep in me. I wanted to know who or what had caused me to no longer have the light in me. It was extinguished. My voice was squashed. I was made to feel insignificant and small.

One moment was this memory, which still plays so vividly in my head. It was a summer I remember well for whatever reason in vivid detail. The smells, the sounds, the taste in the air ... Crazy how memories come back when you least expect them or when you have no desire to remember that moment ever again. Anyway, this was the summer I believe my flame was first dimmed.

I think this was the summer before my parents separated, and it was one of the hottest days I had ever experienced at that point in my young life. The humidity was so thick that you could cut it with a knife. I smelled the moist, stale pavement beneath me as I walked. The smell mixed with the stench drifting up from manhole covers. If you listened intently, you could hear the dirty brown water flowing underground. It sounded like a waterfall I couldn't see.

The rancid garbage piled high in front of the buildings and in the alleys were ominous and scary. Every now and then, a bag would shift and rustle, and I would see a rat poking its head out and disappearing quickly. I heard children playing in the school playground across the street overlapping the sirens from police cars in the distance and the salsa music blaring from fancy, souped-up cars belonging to the drug dealers who would occasionally speed down our street. Groups of men would sit in front of the *bodegas* (grocery stores), playing dominoes or cards while drinking beer and intermittently yelling profanities at each other in Spanish while laughing or cat calling women as they walked by.

I can distinctly remember some friends (I call them friends, but I'm not sure if they were family or just friends) of my parents who lived in the building across our street, in the South Bronx. For some reason, I don't remember why but probably because I was so young, my parents would leave me at this friends' house for hours at a time daily. I don't think my mother was working at the time, so I don't know why I was sent there. The worst part of this memory for me was that what I experienced there wasn't brought on by the adults in that house; they were not the guilty ones who did this. Now that I am an adult, I understand they too were responsible, but I mean that they did not directly subject me to this experience.

These friends had older teenage boys who mistreated me harshly. I was terrified at being left at this apartment, but no one paid attention to little ole Jeanie. I would occasionally cry on the way there as we walked across the street. Unfortunately, the adults in my life chastised me only about crying and told me I needed to be a big girl. They never thought to ask why I was crying.

Once I realized that my cries were falling on deaf ears, I felt absolute doom and sadness as I continued the walk in silence. Just imagine someone walking to his/her death; that was how dreadful it felt for me. I can still distinctly feel the sting of terror somewhere deep in me that I felt then. My parents were so absorbed with their own lives—work stress, relationship issues, and the uncertainty of being new parents perhaps. Who knows? I just know they never noticed the fear in me. My eyes were screaming, *Mom! Dad! Please help me!* but they saw only a crybaby. My parents would drop me off and leave, and it would start almost immediately. I can't even recall where the adults in the house were when this happened, but it didn't matter because it always happened.

On one occasion, these teenage boys painted my face with makeup. When I say they painted my face, I mean that. It wasn't makeup to make me look pretty or to play a cute kids' make-believe game; it was obvious that they were trying to make a fool of me. They would taunt and mock me inflicting suffering on me just for fun. They pointed and laughed at me then teased me once they were done. For a little girl my age, it was very confusing and scary.

Sometimes, they would force me to sit in front of the TV while Archie cartoons were playing but with my head down so I couldn't watch the show. I could hear the show playing but was not allowed to watch at all. If I lifted my head, I was yelled at and mocked even more intensely.

There were other days when after they painted my face, they would hold a mirror to my face while yelling obscenities at me. They forced me to look at myself so I could see the horrible sight, and I detested what I saw. They told me that I looked ridiculous, stupid, ugly, and like a whore, all the while laughing as the mocked me. At the time I had no idea what a whore was, but I knew in my gut it wasn't anything nice. They were very effective too. I felt so shamed, disgusted, and unloved. I felt unnoticed and unimportant.

I couldn't understand then, and especially now that I am a mother myself, how all these adults could be so clueless about the pain I was going through. A two- to three-year-old child should not feel depressed and sad all the time. That was the first time I felt I wanted to die, at least my first memories of those feelings. Even though I did not know how to verbalize these feelings, later on in life I was able to define them. I have nightmares about this memory, and there are blurred parts I can't quite remember or put together to make sense. There has always been something in me that has told me there was more to this, but perhaps I blocked the memory to protect myself from the reality. What was wrong with them? What was wrong with me? Did I make this happen? Was this something I deserved? It was the beginning of the end of my trusting anyone. It was perhaps the beginning of my bad choices too. This was the beginning of my not listening to my own instincts because I didn't even trust myself. Perhaps this was the moment my flame was abruptly snuffed and my soul was changed forever.

As the years passed, I had many more experiences similar to these—some worse, and some at the hands of those who were supposed to love and protect me. As far back as I could remember, I dreamed of leaving home and living somewhere I could be happy and never be hurt again. Often, I fantasized and imagines myself in a faraway place. I thought that if I could escape, I would never have to endure another painful experience. I knew that there was more out there and that I could somehow find my happiness, but unfortunately the feeling of not belonging and self-loathing, followed me everywhere.

* * *

Once my parents divorced, they had their new families, and I didn't fit in, but not that they articulated this to me, it was my own perception based on how I was treated by them. I remember feeling like a visitor in their homes, not belonging completely to one or the other. Imagine one of those dreams where you are watching yourself as a part of a scenario but feeling disconnected from the reality of the experience. I was as an observer, not an active participant – just a visitor. Since no one paid attention to me except to disparage or ridicule me; I began to learn to smile through it all so perhaps they would stop.

* * *

In high school, most people I knew couldn't see past the 325 square miles that made up New York's five boroughs, but I had dreams of life beyond those borders. Perhaps those thoughts came from overhearing conversations between my father and his brothers talking about their travels when they were in the military. Perhaps it was from the books I read. The books I read described places far away that were beautiful, the complete opposite from the musty concrete streets I lived around. I don't know where my desire came from, but I knew I didn't belong where I was. I wanted to be free. I desired an escape from my current reality. I wanted to be a part of a family that loved and needed me. Sometimes I would let my imagination take over as I watched the birds outside my window, wishing I could fly away like they did. Care free and with no obligation to anyone.

Naïve teenager that I was, thought at first that going away to college would be the answer. I went away to college, but that was short lived. Financial struggles coupled with no understanding of how to balance work, study, and my newfound freedom made things very difficult for me. My father was hard on me and his expectations of me were many. As much as I tried to prove my father wrong, I always felt that I could not live up to his expectations so when college fell through, I focused on proving my father wrong in another way. He always said that I was weak, not a true Pizarro, and I began to believe him, but I was determined to do whatever I could to make him see me differently somehow. My goal was for him to see me as a strong, independent, self-sufficient individual separate from our family. Therefore, I enlisted in the Marine Corps. He had served too, and that had made him tough, so I thought it would do the same for me. Little did I know that my yearning to get away from all the dysfunction in my home life would lead my inexperienced self, right into a deeper darkness I never imagined possible nor was I equipped to handle. Honestly, I never dreamed of escaping one trauma just to be unwittingly thrust into another.

* * *

It has taken me a long time to come to terms with what I experienced and come out and tell others that I experienced military sexual trauma and harassment during my service in the Marine Corps let alone share my story with the world. Now, I am ready to share my story and remove the camouflage from this shameful history and turn it into a triumph and a testimony for others to use as their motivation to find their path to healing.

* * *

Trigger warning! For those who are about to embark on the journey into a part of my life, just remember these words may be hard for some to read, and that's ok. Some may want to pass over some parts and read only the parts they need for now. That's ok too. You can read it how it fits your needs.

I do not intend for this book to hurt anyone. Becoming a Marine has been and always will be one of the proudest moments of my life. Till this day, I still carry the pride that I felt the day I walked across the blacktop and became a part of a different kind of family as a US Marine.

Many of you will not understand this, but I don't blame the military for what happened to me. I have learned to compartmentalize the fact that what happened to me was done at the hands of a few twisted and evil individuals, not the military as a whole. Though tragic, my story needs to be told so that perhaps things can change. It needs to be told to give hope to others and show that you can overcome this. It may be intense and traumatic for some, but my wish is that it will give hope to those who do not have hope.

Part I

NIAVE JEANETTE

I

RECEIVING

It takes something special to be a Marine,
but where do these exceptional attributes exist?
Are they in the body? In the mind Or is it
more likely that they're found some place deep?
It is the mindset of a Marine that stands apart.
—US Marine Corps

Whom Is This Book For?

This book is for all my fellow women veterans who have suffered at the hands of sexual assaulters and aggressors. I carried shame, guilt, depression, humiliation, anger, bitterness, and so much more and suppressed it deep inside for no one to see for years. I wore a mask for many years. There were some suicide attempts and mental breakdowns in between as well. I learned to suck it up and move forward as if I were all right. My friends, some family, and coworkers viewed me as someone strong, someone who had it all together. They had no clue I was dying inside. I buried myself in my work or school at first, and then in my children, and last, in being what everyone else wanted me to be for them. I have been there, that black hole of despair.

I have punished myself for things that were not my fault too. I have put myself through situations unnecessarily due to my thinking I needed to make the sacrifice or suffer for my wrongdoings. I was the girl who was never taught to listen to her gut, her intuition, so I doubted and second guessed everything. I was the girl who was taught that her opinions and thoughts were insignificant, so I put everyone else first.

I wanted to write this book for many years, but I continued to hold onto the what-ifs, and I was afraid of the potential blowback form those around me. I was stuck in the idea that if I told my truth, it would be torn apart and scrutinized and I would be judged harshly. I even thought my perspective would be picked apart and those who hurt me in the past would come back to judge me and disparage me yet again. But ultimately, I realized that this was my story and that I wanted to tell it. I needed to tell it all. This is not about them – it's about ME!

I'm telling it from the perspective of my experiences on how I remember it; others can say whatever they want and have their own opinions or perceptions, but I lived this—all the feelings, views, and ideas experienced before, during, and after are all mine, and no one can take that away from me. I will not be silenced any longer by those who hurt me whether family, romantic partners, friends, or strangers. I have taken my power back. I don't even desire or require an apology or to be asked for forgiveness. Ultimately, I have found the peace and continued healing in myself by forgiving the most important person involved in this—myself. God provided me with the forgiveness I needed for me. I pray you find your way to some peace and clarity from reading this book as well.

Another reason I struggled with writing this book was in deciding how to approach it and to whom I would direct it. At first, I feared telling my story just for me because it would open wounds I wasn't sure I was ready to deal with. I did however contemplate using this book as a cathartic way to release the shame I held in for so long. Then as I went through therapy, I realized this book would be all of that and so much more.

It is sad that I walked around a shell of who I was for so many years. Sometimes, I would stay in bed for days because I couldn't face anyone. I was so tired of pretending. I felt like a fraud. I wondered if anyone would ever love me. I lived my life a lie. I smiled through the pain and self-hate during the day just to rush home and hurriedly put my sons to sleep so I could crawl into bed and cry myself to sleep. This is how I lived for so long and it became my norm, but no one had a clue. I was an expert at faking it.

This book is for those of you who need that motivation to live in your truth so you can be happy and recover from your hell. My desire is for this book to give you hope. I want you to know that beyond the pain is joy.

Too often, some people live their lives stuck in a rut of negativity, self-loathing, and doubt. They become engulfed in the misery of their situations and allow the darkness to drag them deeper into despair and low self-esteem. A cloud of uncertainty hovers over them following their every move as if it were a shadow. Some of us may even wear a mask of smiles and strength on the outside as a form of coping. But know that you can remove the mask, wipe away the camouflage, and live authentically.

Military Sexual Assault Statistics

Many statistics point out just how many women have been sexually assaulted, harassed, or abused while serving in the US military. I once believed that discovering that women had gone through experiences similar to mine would ease the pain. I was led to believe that I could feel connection and relief that I was not alone. But it did not. It made me realize how serious this epidemic was. This happens more often than we can fathom.

What would be more helpful is seeing statistics of women who have survived and thrived after being exposed to or having experienced this horrific trauma. Though I will share what I went through and all I endured after, what I want to come out of this book is how we women are stronger than we know. We can come out on the other end of trauma as victorious, thriving warriors. We can turn tragedy into triumph and change our circumstance from being victims to being victors. We can all transform our pain into power.

According to an article published on the website of Hill & Ponton Disability Attorneys (https://www.hillandponton.com/facts-on-military-sexual-trauma-and-statistics/) , military rape law did not begin until the late 1980s. Publicized sexual assault scandals brought the topic of military sexual assault to the forefront and forced legislation, task forces, and commissions to change the military justice system. The DOD issued the Department of Defense Sexual Assault Response policy, now Sexual Assault Prevention and Response Office (SAPRO). However, the most dramatic changes in military justice have occurred in the past ten years.

The following are staggering statistics on military sexual assault and harassment from 2012 to 2020.

- The DOD estimates that approximately 26,000 service members experienced some form of unwanted sexual contact ranging from sexual contact crimes such as groping to rape in 2012.
- RAIIN reports that 6,053 military members reported experiencing sexual assault during military service in FY 2018. DOD estimates about 20,500 service members experienced sexual assault that year. https://www.rainn.org/statistics/victims-sexual-violence.
- Forty-seven percent of female service members experienced sexist behaviors, and 15 percent of male service members experienced sexist behaviors. The percentage of active-duty women who experienced unwanted sexual contact in the past year increased from an estimated 19.3 percent in 2016 to an estimated 28.3 percent in 2018. Department of Defense. 2018. Department of Defense Annual Report on Sexual Assault in the Military.
- According to an article on Military.com (Patricia Kime 2019), "a new survey of active-duty troops has found that the number of sexual assaults in the U.S. military rose by 38% from 2016 to 2018, a dramatic increase that comes despite years of efforts to halt rape and other sex crimes in the ranks."
- In 2018, 20,500 service members were sexually assaulted or raped including 13,000 women and 7,500 men. The rate of sexual assault and rape jumped by almost 40 percent from 2016 to 2018, and for women veterans, the rate increased by over 50 percent—the highest level since 2006.
- Of women who reported a penetrative sexual assault, 59 percent

were assaulted by someone with a higher rank than them, and 24 percent were assaulted by someone in their chain of command.

The vast majority of cases go unreported. A staggering number of victims—76.1 percent—did not report the crime in 2018.

Retaliation is the norm; 64 percent of women who reported a sexual assault faced retaliation, and 66 percent of retaliation reports alleged that retaliators were in the reporters' chains of command. A third of victims are discharged after reporting typically within seven months of making a report. Victims received harsher discharges with 24 percent separating under less than fully honorable conditions compared to 15 percent of all service members.

Low trust and satisfaction in the system. Over one in four victims who did not report feared retaliation from their command or coworkers. Nearly one in three victims who did not report feared the process would be unfair or nothing would be done. Less than half of the female veteran survivors felt supported by their chain of command. (Statistics from the 2016–2019 DOD SAPRO reports and their appendices/annexes, unless otherwise noted. https://www.sapr.mil/reports Updated December 2019).

According to Defense.org, "7,816 reports (were) received by DOD in FY20, 6,290 involved allegations from service members for incidents that occurred during military service."

According to an article written by Kim Doleatto, May 4, 2021, "Sexual assaults and harassment in a single year were linked with 10,000 service members leaving the military within 28 months. According to the Pentagon, 66 percent of service members who reported sexual assault or harassment also reported retaliation, and a third of victims were discharged within seven months of reporting." https://www.sarasotamagazine.com/news-and-profiles/2021/05/military-sexual-assault-legislation.

My period of active-duty service was from February 1991 until April 1997. Unfortunately, neither the DOD nor the Veterans Administration was publishing or fully collecting information and statistics regarding the reporting of military sexual assault or harassment for most of my period of service. In 1994, legislation was first implemented and required the Veterans Administration (VA) to screen all veterans for military sexual trauma (MST), and in 2004, the Veterans Health Administration (VHA) started a national MST screening for men and women in all VA facilities.

In 2010, the first reporting of the results of these screenings came out. If you look at the statistics I have listed, you will see a sickening reality. Though many laws and much legislation have been enacted, statistics did not get much better. Both men and women have continually been reporting experiencing sexual assault and or harassment while serving on active duty at alarming rates. How could that be?

The best way to make change is to shine a light on the ugly facts. We need to speak about our experiences. We need to support each other. We need to use those same tools and training given to us when we became Marines, soldiers, airmen, or sailors to unify and win the battle against this rampant assault on us all. Military sexual assault not only affects the wounded; it also changes family dynamics, friendships, and more.

The more we talk about it and bring it out of the shadows, the less ammunition abusers will have to shame us into silence. So let's win not only battles; let's also win the war.

2

BEFORE THE SHAME

Marines live by a set of enduring core values that form the bedrock of our character. These values guide our actions and bolster our resolve. Honor, courage and commitment lead us to victory over the physical, mental and moral battles faced during combat, or while serving in our communities on behalf of our Nation. These are the values that ensure every fight in current and future battles supports our common moral cause. —Marines.com

The Battle before My War

I was five. My tight pigtails stuck out like two horns turned upside down causing my eyes to squint from their being pulled back by my pigtails. But I wore them proudly. Sadly, that was the only thing I was proud of, and I was so young. In me were constant unrest and fear. I smiled to hide my sadness often, but it slowly crept through me and entered my soul eating at my essence one day at a time. My pain was like a burning campfire being stoked while the happiness in me was being extinguished.

I recall the feeling I had then of no longer being able to endure the pain. I was tired of the aching that dug deep into my soul. It felt like a vice grip on my heart that made my stomach twist and wrench as if I were physically ill. Some days, my throat was so tight that I could barely swallow my saliva. I was more familiar with dread than I was with happiness.

My father was firm and serious. He had served in the US Marine Corps during the Vietnam War. It's hard to grow up on edge not knowing what to expect from one moment to the next. When some family members have demons of which they have not dealt with and project their pain onto you, it can cause anxiety and overwhelming uneasiness.

The expectations of me were very clear: "Pizarro's don't cry." "You stand tall and hold your head up, little girl, and hold those feelings in." "You have no right to feel that way." "You're not a baby, so you need to stop crying." Those words constantly rang in my ears like a broken record. I would hear them in my mind even when they were not being said directly at me. At times, I caught their looks of disappointment, and who wants to disappoint those who love them? I would choke back my sobs and take deep breaths to hold them in. I fought back tears fighting to break free. Some days, I thought I would projectile vomit all over the floor and everyone would then see all the pain I was holding in represented in the splattered puke. They would see all the horror and hurt a five-year-old girl had already lived through.

Quickly after my parents divorced it seemed that someone new was introduced into our family. For as long as I can remember, I always felt like she never liked me. I felt it undoubtedly. I knew it undeniably. At an age when children should be captivated by toys and games, I sensed that person's disdain for me, so my focus became more about how to avoid making her mad. I had no idea how to communicate how I was feeling, how to explain it, or tell anyone. I just knew how much the air was thick with her abhorrence of me almost as if she was jealous of my relationship with my father or perhaps, I was the reminder of the woman he used to be married to and probably still loved.

One day, she was exceptionally angry with me and annoyed. I know I was defiant at times; maybe all children go through this, or maybe it was because my father told me that no one had the right to put their hands on me, but I thought I could do whatever I wanted at times, and I thus tried the patience of some adults. I'm not saying I was a terror, but I initially was vocal about how I expected to be treated. But I was young and had no idea what I was really doing so I am sure I was probably coming off as a smart ass little girl.

I watched how my dad treated people. I observed how cool he was. He wore suits a lot and was always clean cut—his facial hair trimmed and every hair on his head in place. He wore cologne—a lot; I smelled him well before I saw him coming. I thought my dad was the handsomest man in the world. My hero. He was smart and savvy and had the gift of gab. So, whatever he said to me I took as gospel.

Anyway, this family member wasn't very nice to me and especially when my dad wasn't around, and that was often. He would go to work or hang out with his friends and I was left with her. I wasn't used to anyone mistreating me the way she did, so I rebelled in the beginning to show my power. Or so I thought I had power. I felt empowered initially since my father taught me to be a strong little girl. That was what he wanted, right? Well, that's how I interpreted it. So, I had a smart mouth too...I admit. I didn't know if it was because of my sassiness or because I reminded her of someone else, but the hatred she had for me was very clear. I wasn't alone in this belief either; a few others in the family caught her in the act a few times and reported back to my father but he never followed up.

When I was young, I didn't like to eat much, and she enjoyed torturing me regarding that. It was like she relished in seeing my disgust with most food and when I was forced to eat. I was fed strange ethnic meals that only I would have to eat while she ate something else, I wished I could have had instead. So, in defiance I would sit at the dining room table for hours attempting to circumvent having to eat what was on the plate in front of me. I thought I was in control of what went into my body. Wrong. She wanted me to know she was in control in reality. She would scream at me and threaten me. "If you don't eat that food, I'm going to beat your ass!" they would yell.

In my child's mind, I was in control and they couldn't make me eat. "Nobody would make me eat if I didn't want to. My daddy told me so." That's what I would say in my head as I refused to eat. I was wrong. Through the tears that swelled in my eyes and between the sniffles, I shoved spoonsful of food into my mouth as she hovered over me like a giant all the while screaming obscenities at me. I would be slapped a few times, and I was frightened. Why was this person hitting me just to make me eat? My head would spin with confusion as I would attempt to swallow my food and fight the urge to vomit. I would try to finish eating quickly so she would retreat.

Later that night, my dad came home, and I was relieved. I rushed over to him and told him what had happened. He stared at me with a puzzled look and looked over in their direction. "You hit my daughter?" he asked.

This family member attempted to project boldness toward my father and walked into the kitchen as she spewed expletives toward him in a flippant way. He followed her. I smiled because I knew my daddy would protect me and it would never happen again. They yelled back and forth at each other. Then I heard my father say, "How would you like it if someone bigger than you put their hands on you?" A loud thud followed.

I quietly rushed toward the kitchen and peeked in. There she lay on the floor. My heart sunk. This wasn't what I thought would happen. My stomach twisted, and my soul felt as if something were being taken from it. Later, I would learn that that feeling was guilt. Immediately, he bent down and called the her name to see if they were okay. Her eyes fluttered open, and she cried as she held her face with the look of total shock.

No, no, Daddy! That wasn't very nice. That's not what you were supposed to do! was what I thought. I was frozen in fear.

"Don't fucking touch me!" she yelled through their sobs and pushed by to go into another room. "I can't believe you fucking hit me!" He followed her into the other room and closed the door. My heart was thumping. I heard faint, distorted voices yelling back and forth for a while. I sat in the living room with my heart beating so hard I could feel it in my head. Not long after, my father suddenly stormed out of the room and left the house without saying a word to me. He often did that. The front door slammed, and I stood there worried.

The bedroom door opened, and she came into the living room and stared at me intently. As she wiped the tears from their eyes, she bent down close and slapped me hard. She kept swinging, and almost every swing made contact with my face. As I put my hands up to shield my face, I begged her to stop: "Please don't! I'm sorry!" Abruptly, she stopped and through clenched teeth and snarling lips whispered in almost a growl, "Now run and tell your daddy again, but just so you know, every time you do, I'll beat your ass again right after he leaves.

And you know he always leaves." She smirked as she walked away and grab a cigarette to smoke it by the open kitchen window.

My eyes were wide with fear. I believed what was said was true. I no longer felt safe. Whom could I tell now? I was so afraid of the consequences, so I stayed silent. Secrets began for me. From that day on, I never spoke a word of all the abusive ass whippings and the perfuse spewing of vulgarity at me or how often I was told I would never amount to anything and I would just be a *puta* (slut) like my mother.

I often wondered if other little girls lived this way. I watched other children playing and squealing with delight. Jealousy crept in me. They seemed to have no cares. I wondered if they were hiding things also. My envy for them saddened me. I wanted to be them. I daydreamed about playing happily and laughing with my friends. While other children fantasized about fairies and princesses, I visualized having a loving, fun family.

I wanted someone to notice my sadness and make it better. Maybe they would take me away and I would live a joyful existence. Perhaps some loving family wanted a little girl like me and they could take me away. Then I would have a mommy and a daddy together who loved me and laughed with me. Tears would well up in my eyes. I felt my insides changing even though I really didn't understand what that meant. But I smiled though the hurt. I pretended nothing was wrong. I lied to myself and everyone else.

Even when I went to my mother's house on the weekends she showed up, I dealt with another form of torture. I don't believe it was her intention, but she wasn't excited to have me interrupt her single life filled with the freedom to come and go as she desired. Her guilt led her to buy me material things as replacement for the lack of love I experienced. As a small child I interpreted her buying me things as meaning she loved me; but as I grew older, I wished she knew that all I needed was her love and attention.

One weekend in my Junior or Senior year of high school, after speaking to my mother earlier in the week about coming over that weekend, I rode the bus to my mother's house for the weekend. It was early on Saturday morning and I was so excited to be able to do this. My father did not often allow me to travel like that on my own. Once I reached her neighborhood, I walked to her building and entered it. I rang the bell to get into the building but there was no answer. Lucky for me, I knew many people in the building so someone let me in. I made my way upstairs and knocked on her door and patiently waited for her to answer. Nothing. No sounds from inside could be heard either. Sometimes she and my stepfather would take my little sister to the park, so I thought maybe that was where they all were.

I sat on the steps in front of the building and waited for them to return. These were the days where no one had cell phones so all I could do was patiently wait. As I sat there, one of her friends walked up and saw me and asked me what I was doing there. Of course, I told her I was waiting for my mother to come back home. With a puzzled look on her face, she asked "Jeanie do you know where your mother is?" I replied, "well not really." She then informed me that my mother, stepdad and little sister had left for Florida on vacation.

I was floored. My mother wouldn't do this would she? How could she go on vacation without me? She didn't even tell me. Sadly, I got back on the bus and went back to my father's house. Being there didn't make me feel any better either. Actually, they made me feel worse once I was back home and told them what happened. All the things I thought in my mind regarding how selfish she was and horrible it was for her to leave me, were verbalized and amplified by my stepmother. "She never wanted you"; "That's fucked up how she just left you like that". She relished in the act of making me more miserable than I already felt too. This was a moment for her to rub my unhappiness in my face. I cried. A lot.

It was about two weeks before I heard from my mother after this. I addressed her leaving unannounced and somehow the tables were turned on me and I was the disrespectful daughter questioning her mother. I let it go. I figured it was better to drop the subject and conceal my feelings with it. This way, I still had someplace to get away to in order to escape my father's house of horrors. I became so depressed, but I fought to bury any negative feelings in order to survive. I was so weak.

I fantasized about how I would make myself stronger. I knew my father had been in the military; he was proud of that. I thought that if I joined as well, I would be respected and admired as too. Perhaps I would learn to be strong too. Then no one would ever be able to hurt me. I could learn to fight back and scream, "No!" Not my mother nor my stepmother would be able to put their hands on me again. My father would see me through different lenses. Or would they?

* * *

I was eager to get the hell out of the Bronx for so many reasons. I went to a college at Mount St Mary's College all the way up in Newburgh, NY. I was happy I was away from home and on my own. I made it into the pre-med program, but I ultimately found my way right back to where I hated being.

According to the financial aid office, my father made too much money for me to qualify for any assistance. My father refused to pay for my college unless it was the school of his choice. That meant for me to attend college where I chose, I had to apply for grants and loans. I was on my own. No one told me how expensive it would be or how I could get assistance to go to college. I had to figure things out as I went along. I also worked as a lab tech at the school in order to make some extra money so I could buy food and other essentials, but that didn't help.

Boy was I not ready for the responsibility this all entailed. My first taste of freedom, and I crashed and burned. I had no idea how to juggle full-time classes and work and handle my new freedom and experience a social life. My grades suffered significantly; the school sent me a letter of warning during winter break of my sophomore year. The letter stated that all my grants and financial aid had been rescinded. My ability to continue to apply for student loans was also stopped. Unless I could come up with the money for my second semester of sophomore year, I could not return to school. My grades had suffered and dropped significantly to where I was no longer eligible to receive any aide.

I went home on winter break and told my family. It seemed as if no one was worried about the fact that I wanted to stay in school even though they preached about me being required to go to college. I believe they all wanted me to need them, or maybe they wanted me to fail, but I refused to turn to them or fail. Staying in the Bronx, I would probably end up another ghetto statistic. The Puerto Rican girl from the Bronx struggling to work at odd jobs or barefoot and pregnant on welfare. Hell no! That would not be me. No sir! No ma'am! I had to come up with a plan, and I did.

Why I Joined the Marine Corps

The moment that made my decision clear was the night my cousin Noel picked me up from my father's house. My cousin and I were close, like brother and sister. He knew how hard it was to live in my house because he had seen things firsthand himself when we were younger. He even witnessed how I was treated badly. Once we got older, he would occasionally call or drop by and say, "Come on, let's go," just to get me out of the house. He knew they wouldn't say no to him.

That night, we drove around New York City in his work tow truck. It was the blizzard of 1991, and snow was coming down hard. It was so dense it looked like sheets of white cotton stretching down from the sky. We could barely see a foot in front of us as we drove. We would always drive around in his work truck and just laugh and talk all night as he drove. Sometimes, we would stop and get something to eat and talk more. I loved when we would do that because it was my opportunity to get out of that house, occupy my mind with something different, and feel what it would be like to be independent and carefree.

He headed down the Cross Bronx Expressway over to the Henry Hudson Parkway. Strangely enough, the roads were packed with cars, so he bobbed and weaved through the traffic on his way to downtown Manhattan. My cousin knew his way around the city very well, so that was easy for him. Exiting the parkway on 42nd Street, he headed toward Times Square, and then we got stuck. "What the hell is going on here?" he asked. "There are people everywhere. Damn! People don't know how to drive!" For a long moment, we sat at the corner of 7th Avenue and 44th Street. We were facing the building with a digital display of crawling stock market numbers and weather updates and news alerts.

His radio went from playing hip-hop music on Hot 97, to abruptly being interrupted by the announcer talking about Operation Desert Shield and how the Senate had voted on whether we would go to war. The votes were in. I looked up and saw the words "The War Has Begun." My heart sank. The news stated that we were no longer Operation Desert Shield but now Operation Desert Storm. My cousin broke the silence: "Oh shit. It's real now."

I knew right then that I had to be a part of protecting our country. This was how I could get away and do something greater than myself while proving to everyone that I was strong. I had never felt anything as intensely as I did right then. Something in me stirred and awakened. I felt a strong desire to be more than just a daughter, a sister, a Puerto Rican from the Bronx. Everything around me stood still. As corny as it may sound for some, I felt that God was telling me, *You will make a difference in the world. You have gifts and strengths in you that you never knew you had. Believe, and I will be with you along the way.* In that moment, I realized what my purpose was but I kept it to myself for fear of it being picked apart and scrutinized to the point that I might break.

* * *

My father would tell me, "A lady must always carry herself with respect. She should dress in a manner that will make people think, *She's classy.*" It was morning. With my hair blown straight, I dressed as if I were going on a job interview, carrying myself like I thought my father would want me to. I didn't tell my mother or my boyfriend where I was going that day—to the military recruiting station.

It was a cloudy, chilly January day in the Bronx. The snow was almost black due to being mixed with dirt, salt, and whatever garbage was on the ground. I took the bus all the way to the shopping center and got off on the corner where the Grand Concourse crossed Fordham Road. I casually walked toward the military recruiting substation in the middle of the open space on the sidewalk of the overpass to the Grand Concourse.

While walking, I thought, *Wow! I can't believe I'm about to do this.* I was excited and anxious. I pulled the door open, and a bell rang. I saw people inside raise their heads to see who was coming in. All eyes were on me, which made me uncomfortable. I never liked being the center of attention.

A sergeant stood and said, "The Air Force recruiter is next door."

I was puzzled. I replied, "*Ummm*, well, no, I'm here because I want to join the Marine Corps."

That got everyone's attention. It felt like time stood still.

"Really? Are you sure about that?" he asked.

I assumed that perhaps I didn't look the part, but I felt that I was appropriately dressed. Later, I learned that women did not join the Marine Corps often so seeing a woman walk in asking to sign up was rare. I shook my insecurities off and said, "I know what I'm here for, so what do I need to do to sign up?"

He replied, "Well come on in then and have a seat right there, young lady." As he pointed to a chair next to a neatly arranged desk. He had me fill out some forms and asked me a bunch of questions. I took some sort of pretest that helped them determine whether I was suited, and I passed it with flying colors. He then scheduled me to take the official Armed Services Vocational Aptitude Battery (ASVAB) test. I didn't do well on written exams, so I was concerned that I would not do well on this one, but surprisingly I did. Due to doing so well, I was informed that I could practically choose any job field I wanted.

My intention was to join and work in the field of medicine somehow. Unfortunately I quickly learned that the Navy handled the Marine Corps' medical needs, so I had to pick another military occupational specialty (MOS) unless I planned on enlisting in a branch of service that had medical occupations. I was definitely not interested in that. With some reluctance, not knowing any better, I chose to become a military police officer, an MP.

I called or visited the recruiting station every day after narrowing down what the next steps were for me. They probably saw me as the most annoying prospect they had, but I was intent on getting shipped out to boot camp on the earliest date possible. I knew there were procedures to everything, but that didn't deter me. I had the strongest desire to be done with the life I was living and move on to bigger and better things. I signed the original paperwork on January 25, 1991. I was told that I had to wait several months before I left, not something I had wanted to hear. When you initially sign up, you are placed in the Delayed Entry Program (DEP). This is part of the process where they prepare you for what is to come once you actually are shipped out to boot camp. The DEP can sometimes last up to a year in some cases. I did not want to wait that long. So, I showed up at the office or called, every day to check if anything had changed.

On January 29, 1991, my recruiter called and said I might have an opportunity to leave earlier than he had contemplated. Apparently, another female recruit scheduled to ship out discovered she was pregnant during her physical at the Military Entrance Processing Station (MEPS) and they needed a replacement for her. As long as I could pass the physical fitness test and physical exam, I could leave that night.

I rushed over to my father's house to tell him the good news first. I thought he would be happy, but he was not. Why was I not surprised? "What the hell are you thinking?" he yelled. "You can't join the military in the middle of a war! No daughter of mine is going to do something so crazy! You'll never make it anyway!" He looked at other family members in the house and asked, "Can you believe this girl? What the hell's wrong with her? She has no idea what she's gotten herself into!"

My father is notorious for demanding control of every situation. In his mind, only what he believed or stated was fact. I was supposed to follow the plan he intended for me for my life to be successful in his eyes. Since I wasn't following his plans, he sought to find a way to stop me at all costs. He called in a favor from one of his friends of influence from our community and asked him if he could help get me into Syracuse University. This was the school I had really wanted to attend but couldn't afford on my own.

Originally my father refused to help me go there because it was too far away from family and him so he wouldn't be able to control me in the way he wanted. His friend came over, and they planned the next steps of my life as I stood in front of them unnoticed, my voice unheard yet again.

"Seriously, Dad, I'm nineteen and can make my own decisions." This was the first time I stood up to my dad that way and told him what I wanted. He looked at me as if I had lost my mind. Disregarding what I said, he proceeded to negotiate with me. Well, actually, that's a nice way of saying that he told me what I would do next. He said that if I stayed, he would pay for whatever school I wanted to go to, even Syracuse University. His friend said he would work on getting me in there. Their plan sounded nice in theory but something deep inside of me knew better. I shook my head and stood my ground. "No. I'm leaving tonight. I'm enlisting in the Marine Corps"

My father said, "If you do, I'll disown you. You can forget about me being your father"

I walked out the door shakily. Though my heart was racing, and I feared losing my father, my independence was more important. Something in my mind knew that there was a chance he was only offering this olive branch as a way to get me to agree to stay and then nothing would actually happen in my favor. If he did somehow follow through, I also did not want him holding this over my head, because then he would remind me of what he sacrificed for me every chance he got. So, I had to make my own decision. It did not matter the cost. I called my boyfriend and told him I was leaving. He was my first boyfriend and we had plans for our future; I loved him, but I couldn't escape the binds of my father by marrying him to get out of my dysfunctional family situation. Doing that would have bound me to yet another man who would potentially control me. I had to do this for myself. I wanted independence. I wanted to show my father and everyone else who doubted me that I was strong and could do this on my own. I didn't need them.

I headed back to my mother's house. The staff sergeant called later that evening and said he was on his way to pick me up. I needed to be ready to complete my physical fitness test and pass it. There was no turning back now. It was 11:00 p.m. by the time he arrived, and I wondered how I could complete all the things required of me. I can't fail now.

He came to my mother's house in his dress blues. That was the first time I saw a military member dressed in those blue trousers with the red stripes down the side. His blouse (loose fitting waist-length belted jacket worn by the military) looked sharp; it fit him impeccably. On the left breast of his uniform were several ribbons representing his travels, accolades, and experience. Right below them sat an expert rifle badge next to an expert pistol badge. He wore his white cover (military hat), its shiny vinyl bill and frame protruding from the white cloth where there displayed a gold-toned eagle, globe, and anchor emblem, centered on his head to where you could see just the lower part of his eyes peeking out.

We drove across the Bronx to Pelham Bay park. It was so scary and dark that night. The moon was not out, so it made everything seem even darker. This park had a running track inside of which was a field where during the day you could find people having picnics, tossing a ball with their children or working out. On a small patch of undisturbed grass on this field was where I completed my sit-ups. We then walked over to the small children's park on the edge of the field where there stood some monkey bars. Here is where I was to do the timed arm hang. Happily, I completed them both way within the required time limit to pass.

The final part was the run. He saw that I was nervous. My eyes showed my fear clearly. I was uneasy not because I couldn't run but because that park was pitch-black and you could barely see if there was anyone else there. This park was known for shady happenings late at night, everyone from the Bronx knew this. In order to quell my fears, he pointed to his cover and asked, "You see this? I want you to run and keep your eyes on it. Your eyes will adjust in the darkness and you will be able to see it I promise. It will be easy for you to see it in the dark. Just run and follow my cover and you'll be fine."

I did as I was instructed, keeping my eyes fixed on his cover. He made sure to keep within sight. I ran so fast. Before I knew it, I was back in front of him, and he grinned and said, "You're ready. Congratulations. You're on your way to becoming one of the few and the proud."

3

NEW RECRUIT

Marines are trained to improvise, adapt, and overcome all obstacles in all situations. They possess the willingness and the determination to fight and to keep fighting until victory is assured. —Marines.com

Basic Training

Boy I had no idea what I was in for. I had signed up and shipped out so quickly that I had no time to digest the enormity of the decision I'd just made. Normally, those who enlist in the military have some time to learn the customs, prepare mentally and build up their stamina, but I had not been properly prepared on what to expect due to leaving the way I did. Luckily for me I was in good physical shape, but I barely had enough time to pack a bag with my essentials, let alone learn the customs and history of the Marine Corps.

At the MEPS station, we had more forms to sign, and we were sworn in for the final time before leaving. After going through a battery of thorough physical exams and being given all kinds of vaccinations, we were ushered into a van that would take us to the airport in Queens. We arrived at John F Kennedy Airport in Queens NY pretty late. By then, it was night again. I couldn't believe all the time that already passed in a blink of an eye. I had barely had any sleep, so I was functioning on adrenaline alone. We landed in South Carolina and were greeted by a bunch of Marines dressed in their alpha uniforms (the base uniform which consists of a green coat, green trousers with khaki web belt, khaki long-sleeve button-up shirt, khaki tie, tie clasp, and black shoes.) —impressive.

These Marines were drill instructors. They ushered us onto a bus that resembled a school bus. We all boarded the bus, and the drill instructors spent most of the ride to our final destination, giving us instruction on what was expected of us once we reached it. Most of their instruction was essentially screamed at us, and that was shocking. It's strange to have absolute strangers yelling and screaming at you for no apparent reason other than because you existed. Hmmm...familiar.

Looking around at all the unfamiliar faces I was reminded how I didn't know anyone there I could turn to for advice or lean on for support, so I just paid attention and did exactly as I was told. Don't want to draw attention to myself.

Just before we reached the front gate, we were ordered to close our eyes and put our heads down. Well, really, we were threatened that if once we put our heads down and any of us looked up, there would be serious consequences to deal with. Something in me stirred.... My stomach clenched....a flash of memory.... dajavu.

The bus came to an abrupt stop; I could hear a male Marine get on the bus. Someone must have been looking up when they weren't supposed to because he yelled, "I don't know why I see eyeballs looking everywhere!" then he said, "OK listen up! Eyes front. When I say something to you I need a reply from all of you at once as an acknowledgement that you understand my command that says - Sir yes sir! Now say it!" We all repeated his command, but it must not have been clear enough for him because he screamed, "I can't hear you!" We all echoed "Sir yes sir!"

He followed up by saying, "when I give the command, I want you all to get off the bus, grab your gear, and line up on my yellow footprints. Is that clear?" We all replied, "Yes sir!" Suddenly yelling and screaming came from all directions: "Move, move, move get out... get out.... get out of my bus, you nasties!" Everyone tried to scurry off and exit the bus as quickly as possible. Males and females were tripping over each other to get to the underside of the bus, where their personal affects had been stored. Some looked younger than I was and looked frightened, I was too. I took a breath and decided to gather myself; I figured I could wait calmly and retrieve my belongings once the others were done.

Standing beside the open storage compartment I watched drill instructors harass the recruits. I thought, *They have no idea how rough it is. I've been through worse at home. These drill instructors ain't got nothing on some of my family members*, the thought made me laugh loud enough to catch the attention of some of the drill instructors. Not good at all.

A male and a female drill instructor rushed over and screamed at me in unison, "So you think something's funny?" asked the male. "You better move your nasty body and get your trash!" said the female. I was brought back to reality quickly; I grabbed my bag hurried and positioned myself on some yellow footprints painted on the ground beside another recruit at the position of attention like everyone else did. I wondered what the hell I'd gotten myself into. Was my father right? My heart was pounding. Doubt began to creep in.

Just then, a drill instructor started speaking to all of us, "You all are about to embark on a path to becoming a member of the world finest fighting force: The US Marine Corps! The footprints that you are standing on right now have had tens of thousands of Marines stand on them before you. Many of which have sacrificed and given their lives in defense of our corps and our country. Are you prepared to do the same?" We all replied, "Yes sir!"

Boot camp was one of the most challenging things I ever accomplished. However; joining the Marine Corps helped me realize just how strong I was. The best part for me was that I would be a military police officer and that represented strength and power. Right? They were sending me to Lackland Air Force Base in Texas to train there once I graduated from boot camp. I would be someone my father would respect and admire for sure. He would have no choice, right? He would be proud of me. My whole family would be proud of me. Wouldn't they?

I was grateful that males and females were separated in boot camp. Fourth Battalion was where the women trained, ate, and slept. We were taken outside the battalion for church, combat training, weapons training, hand-to-hand combat training, swim qualification, and classes on the history of the military and such. Being separate allowed us to focus on the task at hand—no distractions from the hard work.

Halfway through training, I injured my back while manipulating the obstacle course. They required us to challenge ourselves with completing it as quickly as possible. It is 300 feet (approximately one-half mile) from the first obstacle down to the last, once you have completed it. It is meant to test your endurance, strength, and mental fortitude. We competed against each other but ultimately it was against ourselves. Our drill instructors made us practice every chance we could.

* * *

This day was grey and humid. A typical day in South Carolina really. It was as if it wanted to rain but the rain was sort of stuck. The clouds were low, and the air was thick. The obstacle course had many parts of which we needed to learn to manipulate and tackle in order to conquer it. At first, I didn't think it was too bad just by looking at it, as I thought it looked like an adult-sized playground. To me, the only difference was that I was being timed. Some of the obstacles were built with large pieces of wood and others were mixed with wood and metal bars.

As I always had the many other times I attempted the obstacle course, this day I made it over the first two obstacles easily. When I reached the third obstacle, I jumped off the log so I could reach the metal bar, then I swung my feet to catch the bars positioned vertically in front of me and parallel to the ground. The objective of this obstacle was for us to shimmy across the bars until we reached the other side and then jump down. Unfortunately, those bars were metal, and in the weather we were practicing in, a light coating of mist made them very slippery. So, when I jumped and caught my feet on the metal bars and started to shimmy across, my hands lost their grip and my feet slipped simultaneously. I fell straight down right on my back and had the wind knocked out of me. As I was flopping on the ground from the pain and trying to catch my breath, a drill instructor screamed, "No one told you to stop, recruit! Get up and try again!" I jumped up and tried but was not successful. I was unable to finish the obstacle course that day.

Because I was worried I wouldn't be able to complete my training, I pushed myself past the pain so I could get through the rest of our rigorous physical training. Thankfully, I completed everything necessary to proceed. I even graduated as one of the squad leaders of my platoon. Damn, I was proud of myself.

* * *

I worried that my father wouldn't come to my graduation from boot camp due to how he responded to the way I left. I got letters and postcards from home, but the ones he occasionally sent me were not very uplifting nor supportive. To my surprise though, he came with my stepmother. My mother also came, accompanied by my boyfriend, little sister Kristina, and favorite aunt Patricia. Happily, we all celebrated my graduation together. Now I was a different person. *Will they notice that?* I wondered.

My mother immediately noticed the difference in me. She cried when she saw me. She said I reminded her of my father when he came back from Viet Nam. My aunt was so happy for me. She reminded me that she knew I could do it all along. My aunt was always supportive and motivating. Right after I graduated my father walked up to me on the parade deck and said, "I'm so proud of you" with a smile on his face of approval. Him saying this made me feel like I had finally conquered my goal.

MOS School

After about thirty days of being home on annual leave, I returned back to the base where I graduated from boot camp. Unfortunately, I had lost my assignment for MP training due to my back injury, so my MOS was replaced with administrative clerk. I was instructed to return to Parris Island to wait for the next administrative class to begin. Boy was I pissed. I hadn't joined the military to be a glorified secretary, but I had to deal with it and do my best. I was not looking forward to being their version of a secretary, but what choice did I have at this point? So, I just put in my mind that if I had to do this, I was going to be the best damn administrative clerk they ever had.

Eventually after about a month or so was sent to Camp Johnson, a base in North Carolina, where administrative clerk courses were taught. A lot had changed for me since I had joined the Marine Corps. My boyfriend and I had decided to break up; we did so on good terms right before I left back to South Carolina. He had no intention of following me as he had family responsibilities of his own back in New York. I was okay with his decision as I respected the fact that he made his family a priority especially since we remained friends.

While at MOS school, I met Jonathan as I will call him, the first person I had a romantic relationship with. We were inseparable the whole time at Camp Johnson. My gut felt something was off about him, but I ignored it. I was enamored by him and the attention he gave me. It was passionate and intense, and we shared a lot. I suppose I was swept off my feet, to say the least, by a military man who portrayed himself to be all the things I thought I needed.

I graduated from administrative clerk school in the summer of 1991. Johnathan had not completed his MOS training yet, so he stayed in North Carolina; once I graduated, we didn't see each other for a while after I left the base. During our time apart, we talked on the phone often. He traveled to New York to meet my family soon after. Our plan was that we would get married once we knew where he would be stationed once he graduated from his MOS school. Unfortunately, once he graduated, he was told he had to leave for Japan for the next year. We believed we would make it work somehow.

My orders sent me to Hawaii, where I was stationed at Marine

Corps Air Station on Kaneohe Bay. I was assigned to a unit that was considered a combat support unit, Brigade Service Support 1, in their administrative office. I couldn't wait to check into my new duty station. I imagined exploring and experiencing all the things I dreamed about when I was younger. The Puerto Rican girl from the Bronx was finally on her way to greater things.

4

STRENGTH TEST

It is the quality that empowers Marines to exemplify the ultimate in ethical and moral behavior: to never lie, cheat, or steal; to abide by an uncompromising code of integrity; to respect human dignity; and to have respect and concern for each other. —HQ Marine Corps

First Duty Station—Shame Shows Its Face

Hawaii was beautiful. The air smelled clean, and it was so green, a green I had not seen in New York. This green reminded me of looking through HD glasses. Everything was crisp, and all the beautiful colors on the flowers were amplified. I was so excited when I got there. I planned on doing all the things I could never do back home. I wanted to explore, experience and live all there was to offer in Hawaii.

All the other Marines given orders to the same base as I was, were instructed to report to their perspective units once we had gone through the orientation process. I couldn't believe that I would live in such a beautiful foreign place for the next three to four years. Luckily for me, I had at least twelve of my administration classmates with whom I could share this experience. I now appreciate how a lot of the people I met in the Marine Corps ended up being my new family. My fellow classmates and I stuck close together for at least the first week until we were sent to different units across the base. Two males and I were sent to our unit together to work at the administrative office. Many of us remained friends even once we were separated.

Even though I struggled with the fact that I had never wanted to be a glorified secretary in the Marine Corps, I settled into the idea and figured I had better make the most of it; I decided to be the best administrative clerk I could be. I would make sure to learn everything I could and do my job better than anyone else.

Few people know how difficult it is to be a woman in a man's world especially in the Marine Corps. I was thrust into a combat support unit with thousands of males surrounding me some of which still had old school views and values when it came to women in the military. Coming from NYC, I was used to the catcalls, but this environment was much different. Some of these males were aggressive with their attentiveness and advances toward women subtlety. I had to quickly become hardened and ignore their advances using an approach much different than how I dealt with men in New York. I had to carry myself different from the way other women carried themselves too. Quickly, I learned if you showed even a small reaction, somehow that made them believe you were interested in them; then, it gave them the liberty to pursue you even harder.

I also quickly learned how some male Marines perceived females in the military—as Bible-thumping, hard-core or as easy and willing to sleep with anyone. I chose to be the smart-mouthed, hard-core who tries to do everything better than the men did; I thought that was the best way to assimilate while still being respected. I also figured that I could keep the men at bay this way. I turned myself into a mean, bad-tempered Marine Corps woman. Slowly, most backed up from me, and the attention slowed to a crawl. I liked that.

I consistently kept a serious face and tried not to make eye contact with the male Marines who seemed to want to talk to me. Some would approach me with big smiles trying to hit on me forcefully while others would try to strike up casual conversations hoping I would engage them and give them a chance. I was naïve, so sometimes, I couldn't tell the difference.

Andrew (I'm not using his real name) was different I thought. I had met him in the barracks when I first checked in. He was fairly attractive, the kind of guy I might date if I had been available, but I had a boyfriend, so I wasn't interested in him that way. In the past, I had male friends that were strictly platonic so to me, having him as a potential friend was no different. Something was different about Andrew, but I couldn't put my finger on it. The other guys didn't like him much, but

I didn't know why. I knew little about him but since he was my fellow Marine, what harm was there in getting to know him? Honestly, I wasn't thinking anything seriously so, to me, everything was normal.

He was smooth and charming. Casually, he would say only hello as I passed him. After several times of his doing this, I nodded in acknowledgment of him and smiled weakly when we saw each other. I tried not to give him the wrong impression. I didn't want him to think I was attracted to him in a romantic way. We had several encounters that way for about four to five days until we began to talk casually. He appeared innocuous, and on occasion, he even made me laugh. Someone who makes you laugh can't be threatening, right? Eventually, I would stop and have short conversations with him, and he seemed easy to talk to, so I let my guard down. In my naïve mind, I believed the Marine Corps would never have enlisted anyone who was dangerous. We spent time together with a few other Marines or out in the open in public places.

Andrew had been in Hawaii longer than I had been, so he showed me around a lot. He even invited me to church. He really couldn't be that bad, right? A few weeks after I arrived, I was promoted, and he invited me to a beach party in town. Harmless. I went. I thought he was charismatic and respectful, someone good to have as a friend.

We discussed my boyfriend; we had several conversations about Johnathan and the plans we had for the future. From my perspective, Andrew never even hinted that he was interested in me romantically, so I felt at ease since I had no intention of any romantic relationship with anyone else either. In retrospect, didn't think I gave off a vibe of anything to the contrary. In my mind I was only interested in meeting other Marines and enjoying my time in Hawaii. Part of me was lonely, yes. But, I yearned for the connection with someone to be a friend and just let loose without worry, and Andrew seemed like someone I could potentially do that with.

Andrew told me we would be meeting some other military members from our unit at this beach party. He drove us to Waikiki Beach, what a beautiful place. We got there right before sunset, and I was caught up with seeing the bright orange sun glistening as it was setting over the clear blue waters of the ocean. My gut nudged me slightly making me aware that no one at this party seemed familiar, but I ignored the prod. I didn't really know many people so that's not out of the norm. Is it?

We talked for a long time. Evidently, he was trying to keep my focus off the fact that we were not really at a beach party with other Marines from the base as he had told me. Our conversation was easy and relaxed; at some point I became so engulfed in the conversation I didn't pay attention to anything else. We laughed and smiled and talked; it all seemed innocent. He never tried anything remotely aggressive like other guys had, so my guard remained down. It started getting dark. Occasionally, some people walked by and said hello, but they never stopped to talk to us.

We were sitting on a concrete picnic table off to the side of where some people were gathered. They were playing music, dancing, talking, and laughing. Andrew asked me if I wanted something to drink, and I said yes. While he was gone, I watched moonlight reflecting off the waves right before they crashed and surged—peaceful and mesmerizing. Andrew came back with two opened wine coolers and handed one to me. I took a sip as he watched me intently, and we continued our conversation. We talked about life, work, friendships, relationships, religion, goals in the military ... I sipped some more.

I woke up the next morning in my barracks room groggy and feeling strangely fuzzy. So, how did I get here? I was wearing my light grey cotton shorts jumper and white sneakers. My shorts jumper was slightly wet, and I found sand in my pockets. I wondered how that had happened too because I didn't remember sitting on the beach. I couldn't remember anything actually. My body hurt in places it shouldn't have. Feeling odd and trying to remember the previous night, my stomach sank because I had this nervous feeling that something bad had happened, but I couldn't remember what it was. My head was killing me, and I didn't know why. The only thing I remembered was drinking some of that one wine cooler Andrew gave me. I can remember getting to Waikiki beach, but I could not remember anything past sitting on that concrete picnic table talking to Andrew.

I showered, dressed, and headed to the chow hall racking my brain trying to remember what had happened the previous night, how I had gotten back to my room, who had brought me back, and what had happened. My head was spinning. My stomach was having a sinking sick feeling I couldn't shake. I never made it to the chow hall. I kept on walking and ended up at the bleachers near a field away from where anyone would see me. I sat and tried hard to retrace my steps the previous night but couldn't. Tears streamed down my face. I was scared and confused.

Monday, I went to work. As I walked across the street from my barracks, I felt uncomfortable stares. I usually didn't pay much attention to that stuff because I didn't want anyone to think that I was full of myself. I kept my eyes focused on my office and kept walking straight. People were treating me differently, but I didn't know why. Perhaps I was paranoid due to not knowing what had happened days before, so I was projecting my fears. Something was not the same. I felt it.

Days passed, and I felt more and more sick. A nauseating feeling lingered in me and ebbed and flowed off and on daily. An unfamiliar feeling. Andrew occasionally tried to stop and talk to me, but I kept the conversation short and would walk away. I don't even know why, but I never got the nerve to ask him directly about what happened that night. Perhaps I was afraid to know the answer? Strangely, he began to make slightly lewd comments about my belonging to him, but I shrugged it off as him just trying to be funny.

I began to have very vivid dreams—nightmares—where I was at the beach and someone was on top of me and I was screaming *Stop!* in my head, but all I managed to get out was a weak, "No ... Please don't." I heard waves crashing and a male whispering in my ear, but I couldn't quite hear what he was saying. They were flashes of visions. None were complete, but they were enough to startle me. The salt air was dense and moist. I smelled suntan lotion and ocean. I would wake up abruptly, breathing hard and thinking I had sand on my hands from trying to pull away from the assailant in my dream. In my dream, this unknown man had me pinned onto the sandy beach and I struggled to get away but failed.

I hated those dreams. They confused me. They scared me. I didn't know why I kept having these horrible nightmares. Sometimes, I woke up in tears feeling panicked, disoriented. Too embarrassed, I didn't tell a soul. I wondered if I was going crazy. Had something happened? Was I reliving something I had experienced but couldn't remember? I wanted to keep this to myself so no one would think anything was wrong with me. I didn't want to lose everything I worked so hard to achieve. In the military, it didn't take much to tarnish a woman's career, especially one as titillating or salacious as a potential sexual indiscretion – I still was not able to call it what it was. Rape. Sexual assault.

Shortly after, I befriended some female Marines and started to feel a little better. I tried to forget about that night and the repulsive nightmares. Some rumors were circulating that Andrew had slept with me. Some people were even bold enough to ask me directly, but I looked at them puzzled as if they were crazy and would say, "Hell no!" This was the first time while in the military that I had been accused of doing something I hadn't done, so I didn't know how to handle it. I isolated myself. I never even told my newfound friends what I was struggling with. Once, however, I mustered up the courage to ask Andrew why he was saying those things, but he would just smirk at me and walk off.

It became a regular occurrence for me to have nightmares and flashes of the mysterious male on top of me. Sometimes, the dreams were so vivid that I would wake up in a cold sweat. Most of these dreams were of me on the beach and him groping and tugging at my clothes.

He was kissing me, and I was telling him, "Stop, I have a boyfriend."

He said, "*Shhhh ...* Don't worry." As he groped and molested my breasts and vaginal area.

I would wake up scared and even more confused and disoriented. I was sick to my stomach. I believed I was losing my mind. Johnathan would call me from Japan often, and we would talk, but I felt different. Things had changed. Johnathan sensed the difference in my voice even though I tried to disguise it. I struggled with what to say to him. I couldn't articulate what I was going through. I felt so wrong...dirty even. I didn't feel safe telling him anything. I actually couldn't explain it to myself. The only word that kept creeping into my head was shame. If I hadn't gone with Andrew, this would have never happened. It's all my fault. So, I lied to Johnathan; I told him that I was seeing someone else and that we should break up; it made him furious enough to call me a few expletives and then he hung up the phone. (We didn't speak again until about twenty years later, but that's a story for my next book). I was broken. I walked around a shell of who I was, in a haze of reality. I was determined to find a way to make this all go away though.

A few weeks later, I learned there was a group from our unit returning from Iraq having been deployed for Desert Shield and Desert Storm. I was introduced to a bunch of them who worked in my office, and that included a Marine I will call Mark. (His name has been changed for privacy reasons.)

In the mornings before work, we had to police call—*pick up trash around the barracks area grounds and grass.* I was intently doing my part when I felt someone staring at me. It was Mark. He was standing near the barracks with a few other Marines and he was smiling at me. I hated being gawked at especially by a bunch of men.

I asked him, "Do you need a ruler?"

Mark frowned and looked at me baffled but replied, "Huh? What do you mean?"

I said, "So you can measure my tonsils since you're all in my mouth!"

His friends and some other Marines standing nearby burst out laughing. He shook his head and said, "Okay, you got me," with a laugh.

At that point, I was even more defensive. I wasn't too nice to him, at first. I had no interest in dealing with any more shenanigans, so I wasn't amused at all. Fortunate for him, eventually I softened up when I had to interact with him since we worked in the same office. Our relationship developed to the point that we were spending a lot of time together. Since we worked together, it was convenient and easy to get to know him. I felt safe with him for sure, especially because lots of other Marines knew him, especially the higher ranking ones as well as the fact that he had many friends.

We became comfortable with each other as friends at first. On several occasions, Mark mentioned to me that he had heard rumors about my being in a relationship with Andrew. Of course, I denied it because it wasn't true. This made me very frustrated. I hated having to constantly defend myself, but this was the way it worked in this environment I suppose. Fortunately for me, most of the times I was accused of being with Andrew, I was out with Mark off base somewhere or hanging out in his room with other Marines talking, watching them play spades, or watching movies. Eventually, the rumors died down or people just chose to ignore the whispers.

About a month or so after the beach incident, I was still feeling sick, so I went to sick call - *our medical clinic* - and told them how awful I felt. They sent me to the main hospital to get checked out and get some bloodwork done. To my disgust, I was told that I had contracted a sexually transmitted disease. This wasn't the worst part either. On top of it all, I was also pregnant. How could that be? I hadn't had sex with anyone since Johnathan, and that was long before I reached Hawaii. Time stood still for what seemed like forever. Is this real? I wanted to die. I was embarrassed and shocked as well. I was almost positive Johnathan didn't give me a disease either. How could I be pregnant? I had had my period at least once since I had arrived in Hawaii too and once before I got there.

Then it hit me like a ton of bricks. Oh my goodness! Those dreams were not dreams at all. I numbly walked from the hospital to the barracks without even realizing I had done so. Anger rose in me like water boiling in a tea kettle. Mark saw me and shouted, "Hey! Is everything okay? Are you good?" My anger prevented me from responding for fear that if I did, I might burst into tears. So I kept walking. I found myself in front of Andrew's barracks room door. Mark was still calling my name. Like a faint echo, his voice sounded distant and hollow.

I pounded on the door and shouted, "I know you're in there! Open up!"

A few seconds later, the door swung open, and Andrew smiled that stupid grin he always made and said, "What's up? How can I help you?" in his slithering voice.

"You bastard!" I shouted.

"What are you talking about?" he asked.

"You know exactly what you did to me!"

Immediately I started hitting him wildly and one of my swings landed and busted his lip. By then, Mark had reached me and grabbed me so I couldn't continue to pummel Andrew. "Stop!" Mark yelled as he pulled me away.

"That son of a bitch did it! Oh my God he did it!" I shrieked as I cried. I knew what I wanted to say but the words wouldn't form so all I could do was scream obscenities at him from being repulsed. With all the commotion I caused, the staff sergeant on duty heard my shouts, came over, and asked, "What's going on here?" He saw Andrew holding his bloody mouth and asked, "Who did this?" as he looked at me being held back by Mark and crying. "Was it you?" he asked me.

I started to say yes, but Andrew interrupted me. "We were just playing around, and I hit my mouth. It's all good here, Staff Sergeant."

The staff sergeant looked at us suspiciously and said, "Everybody go about your business and disburse, or I'll write you all up."

Mark pulled me away and guided me into his room. I collapsed on his bed crying even more. He let me cry and stood there silently not knowing what else to do for me.

Once I gathered myself, Mark asked, "Do you want to talk about it?"

I ended up explaining to him that I believed I had been sexually assaulted. I was embarrassed to say I didn't have a clear memory of it, but my dreams and what I had learned gave me the clarity I needed to be sure that that was what had happened. Even more embarrassed, I told him I was pregnant and had a sexually transmitted disease. I thought he would be repulsed by me with this information.

Instead, he gently put his arms around me and said, "It'll be okay. You'll be fine. What do you need me to do?"

As harsh as it may sound, I replied, "I need to get this thing out of me" as I started to cry again. I couldn't wrap my head around the idea of carrying the child of someone who had violated me in that way. My worst nightmare had become a reality. If I didn't do something to make all of this go away, I would die.

Once I returned to work, I told my master sergeant privately about my situation. Not all of the horrid details thought. I didn't tell her about the beach and what Andrew had done to me. I still couldn't put the words together to say the truth. Shame held me hostage. I just wanted to let her know that I needed to have an abortion, but I didn't know how or where to go. Reluctantly, she helped me find a Planned Parenthood office on the island. She said I needed to have someone take me there and bring me back. She explained that I would not be in either an emotional or physical space to do it alone. So, I asked Mark, he was the only person I could trust at this point, and he agreed to take me.

The morning of my appointment with Planned Parenthood, Mark drove me there and patiently waited for me. Once the procedure was done, I felt just awful. I thought once it was over, I would feel relief but that wasn't the feeling I was having at all. I couldn't believe I had gone through something that I would have to deal with for the rest of my life. The memory would never go away. My stomach hurt badly. Mark took me straight to the barracks and let our master sergeant know I had made it through ok and was in bed resting.

The next day, however, I woke up in excruciating pain and began to bleed uncontrollably. My body felt like it was burning up. I had a fever; I couldn't think straight either. Mark came to check on me during his lunch break. I was so out of it and disoriented, and I was crying out in pain. I recall at one point crying out for my mother.

From what I was told, Mark ended up telling the person on duty that something was wrong with me, and they called an ambulance; I was rushed to the hospital. At the hospital, I learned why I was in so much pain – the diagnosis was a septic abortion and they had to perform a dilation and curettage procedure. It is also called a D&C, which is a surgical procedure in which the cervix is dilated so that the uterine lining can be scraped with a spoon-shaped instrument to remove abnormal tissues trapped inside the uterus. They needed to remove some dead tissue that still remained in my uterus from the improper abortion I received earlier. I had to be treated for the infection as well via IV fluids. Then I was sent home a few days later.

In the military, word gets around easily; people talked about what had happened to me. Though they really didn't have all the details, they knew enough to talk. I believe basically what they did know was that I had had an abortion and it had made me sick. I suppose they thought it belonged to Mark since we were at that point considered an item. We let people believe what they wanted to believe. As far as I knew, Mark corrected no one.

Mark asked me several times why I did not want to report what had happened to me at the beach. I told him I was too humiliated and mortified to describe to anyone what had happened especially because I couldn't remember how it happened in the first place. I thought perhaps that I had given Andrew the impression that I was interested in him. I thought maybe because a part of me found him attractive, maybe subconsciously I wanted to do it. Maybe I had led him on. Perhaps I deserved all that happened since I should have never gone anywhere alone knowing that I had a boyfriend. I didn't think anyone would believe me. I had willingly gone with him; I trusted him. I had a boyfriend, so I had no business going with some guy I barely knew anywhere alone. I felt that it was all my fault and that I had deserved what had happened. I couldn't tell anyone. I made Mark promise he wouldn't say anything either, and he agreed to keep my secret.

Once Andrew discovered that I had had an abortion he came looking for me. He had the nerve to corner me one day when I was alone in my barracks room and chastised me.

He said, "I can't believe you actually killed my baby!"

I looked at him baffled and shocked. Was he telling me this as if what he had done was something I had willingly participated in? Am I really hearing him admit that he was the one?

My heart slowed for a moment, as I told him calmly, "I suggest you get the hell away from me before I beat the shit out of you. If you know what's best for you, you'll stay away from me and stop telling stories and spreading lies too. Don't fuck with me."

He chuckled as he walked away. I was shaking. I rushed into my room for safety and shut the door so he wouldn't see how scared I really was. I collapsed into my chair.

Several months passed. I made sure I never walked alone anywhere. I had nightmares regularly, so that was something I mentally prepared myself for every night. Everything startled me easily; I jumped at the slightest sound, and I fought with Mark over the littlest things. I was angry all the time and would burst out crying out of the blue. Most days, I felt a shell of my former self. My relationship with Mark was strained. He had his own issues; he was young and had no clue what he was dealing with when it came to me, but he was a good guy. He tried desperately to make me feel better, but he didn't know how. How could he have when I had no idea what I needed myself?

I don't remember how or when, but I was instructed to report to some lawyer to discuss being a character witness for Andrew. Rumor was that he had held an underage girl, the daughter of a sergeant major, against her will in the barracks and had sexually assaulted her for several days. People were whispering about how he had given some girl the date rape drug too. Though I didn't know how true it was, I felt absolutely sick to my stomach. Maybe this was why I couldn't remember the details of that night. Was I also a victim of his treacherous schemes? This poor girl became another one of his victims. I could have prevented it if only I had spoken up. Shame flashed on my face again.

Now, he wanted me to be a character witness for what? Oh my goodness ... I wouldn't talk to anyone and be this crazy guy's character witness. Absolutely not! Andrew was insane to even suggest I could be that for him. Did he suggest me to his lawyers? I ignored the request at first, but I quickly learned I couldn't refuse it while on active duty.

Due to my refusal to appear, they reported me to my master sergeant. She called me to her desk and explained that I was to report to the legal office immediately. They interviewed me, and though most of it is a blur, I remember telling them, "You really don't want me to get on that stand and be his character witness." They asked me a few specific questions, and my responses must have scared them. The next thing I remember was being told that they would not need me. I was sent away.

A few weeks after that, I was in the office working when my master sergeant called me over to her desk as she usually did when she needed me to do something. She told me that Andrew was being escorted to our office so he could be processed out and dishonorably discharged. Apparently, whatever charges they had against him had been proven. I was shaking and sweating. Blood rushed to my face. Shakily, I said, "Yes, Master Sergeant," and unsteadily walked back to my desk.

A few minutes later, two military police officers escorted him into the office shackled in chains and wearing an orange jump suit. They walked with him until he reached my desk, and he sat. They gave him his privacy—as if he deserved that—and posted themselves a few feet from my area. My hands were sweaty, but I quickly tried to get his paperwork together.

Every now and then, I scanned the office looking for Mark; I was desperate for a source of strength. When our eyes met, he would nod and give me a look of support, of reassurance. I knew I could make it through that moment. I had to ask Andrew several questions in order to complete his paperwork. Under his breath, he kept whispering to me.

One time he whispered, "Are you going to miss me?" I was stunned.

I didn't know what to say. The room suddenly started spinning. I should have screamed out and reported him, but I was frozen. My hands had a mind of their own so without even thinking I hurried his paperwork so I could get him out of there.

Once he left, I scurried to the bathroom while struggling to hold back my cries. As soon as I entered the bathroom, my heaves took over and I threw up as I cried. But at least he was gone. They escorted him to the Honolulu Airport, where he would fly home and be met by the police there. I was relieved. The shame still lingered in me though. I wondered if he would ever really be gone.

Months later, my relationship with Mark developed into something more serious. We still struggled though. Well, honestly, I struggled. I had outbursts and yelling matches with him. I felt so defeated on certain days. I blamed him for my misery, but in hindsight, I realize I was miserable about everything that had happened but never resolved. He was the closest person to me, so he became my emotional punching bag. A rollercoaster of emotions consistently resided in me.

Eventually, I got pregnant by Mark. Initially, I was sad; I thought my world would end. What kind of mother would I be? There was no way I could take care of a child. I didn't even want to have children. I was terrified. Mark asked me to marry him when I told him I was pregnant, but I wasn't willing to trust a man to take care of me. In my mind, him asking me to marry him was a knee jerk response to me being pregnant and not that he wanted to spend the rest of his life with me. I was scared. Everyone I had trusted to protect and love me had ultimately betrayed me, hurt me, or left me. On several occasions, Mark cheated on me, but I accepted him still. I know we were young; he was a decent guy who would have ultimately done the right thing, but I couldn't let go of my fears and try because all I could see was failure. My failure. I pushed him away and acted as if I didn't need him. Every chance I got

I reminded him that I could do it on my own. I was lying. My anger continued to bubble up and explode towards him. Before he could leave me, I would make him leave. Several months after discovering we were having a child, he was transferred to a duty station off the island. To me, that was a sign to let him go, and he let me go too.

Once Mark was gone, I was alone and learning to maneuver things on my own as always. I was always meeting people at my job. Over a year prior to all my drama, I was introduced to Steve. We had lost contact once he transferred to another unit on the other side of the base. Steve and I bumped into each other as he was about to leave for his scheduled deployment overseas. I was about eight months pregnant then. We exchanged phone numbers and started a long-distance relationship. Yes, stupid, but I was young and had no idea what I was doing. I was trying to maneuver my way through life one day at a time. I believe now that I was searching for my happily ever after. He was deployed on a ship for six months in the middle of the Pacific. Okay, I know—What the hell was wrong with me?

Unfortunately, I didn't have the greatest examples of successful and functional relationships nor did I have anyone to turn to for advice. Anyway, we communicated several times a day for hours at a time and developed what I believed was a real connection. It was safe for me that way too.

In January 1993, Steve returned to Hawaii, and I was ecstatic to start my new life with him. Everything seemed perfect when Steve got to my house. Just my luck; the first time we were together intimately, I got pregnant. Sadly, on top of that, I discovered that all the while he was pledging his love and loyalty to me, he was also pledging the same to someone else. What the hell was wrong with me? I couldn't get a break! Well, that didn't work either.

The worst part for me was that I discovered all his indiscretions after I was pregnant with our son, so what could I do at that point? I confronted him, but he was defensive and aggressive; denying it all. The other woman would call and harass me and tell me how much he loved her and not me. After weeks of going back and forth with him regarding his cheating with the other woman, I couldn't take it anymore and I kicked him out. Without much of a battle, Steve left me and married the other woman not long after while I was five months pregnant - and on my birthday! Oh, that stung badly. Believe it or not, Steve continued to tell me he would fix everything so we could be together. A totally dysfunctional relationship. Though I knew this was a bad situation, I couldn't find it in myself to tell him no. I held on without knowing why. All the while, he manipulated me and his new wife. Both of us were being played and we knew it but allowed it to happen. At that point, I believed that no one would want me so I might as well take what I could get. I was about to be a mother of two children by two different men. To the outside world, that didn't look good. So, I held on. I let him come and go between me and her. Smiling my way through this completely dysfunctional situation. Pretending I could handle it. Since she was tolerating the circumstances then why shouldn't I? Absolutely insane!

In the midst of this, I met Darius. We worked together. I gave him a hard time, but he ignored my boorishness. He wasn't pushy or aggressive in the slightest way, but what did I know? I wasn't the greatest judge of character and my experience proved it. Somehow, he made it past my wall of anger, bitterness, and distrust and became my friend—a real friend. I didn't want to get involved in another potentially dead-end relationship. What the hell could he want with a pregnant woman on her way to having two children by two different men? That would have been insane, right? He was younger than I and I just couldn't see him having his life disrupted and ruined by my mistakes.

I didn't let him into my heart, but I let him in my circle of trust. Darius was kind and gentle and especially helpful with my kids. He spent a lot of time at my house. Darius helped me so much, and I appreciated how he had no expectations. He watched the boys for me and let me have time to take care of things around the house. I taught him how to change their diapers and care for them. He seemed to really enjoy spending time with me and the boys. I was surprised that he did it without conditions. Can you believe he even was the first man to carry my youngest son when I gave birth? He came to the hospital and picked us up once I was discharged and took us home. I couldn't understand what he saw in me, I was so messed up and once he saw the truth he too would walk away or find someone better. So eventually, I pushed him away.

I needed a way out. I couldn't handle any of this. I didn't trust my decision making. All I saw was my mistakes. What would my children think of me if I allowed myself to stay? How could I look myself in the mirror every day and respect what I saw? Steve had turned me into a woman I hated—a mistress. The only thing I could think of was getting out of Hawaii and away from Steve. He continued to show up at my house unannounced demanding and expecting things that only a boy-friend or husband should. He had a key to my house and refused to return it under the guise that he wanted to be able to check on me and our son. I knew that he really only wanted to make sure no one else was taking his place, but little did he know I was too tired to even entertain the thought of anyone else.

Though I was too weak to stand up to him, I realized that the dys-function had to somehow end. Steve's wife knew he would be at my house and would call to ask for him to come home. That was foolish-ness on so many levels. We were both being played, and we allowed it. I needed to somehow get away from Steve and the madness I allowed him to put me through.

5

TESTED AGAIN

Courage is the mental, moral and physical strength ingrained in Marines. It carries us through the challenges of combat and aids in overcoming fear. It is the inner strength that enables us to do what is right, to adhere to a higher standard of personal conduct and to make tough decisions under stress and pressure. —Marines.com

Second Duty Station:

Shame Has a Follow-Up, a Sequel, and a Trilogy

It paid off for me to end up as an administration person. I did my due diligence and learned the rules and regulations and the names of those I needed to contact in order to get things done right. I was grateful that I was smart in that sense. I reached out to my career planner and got him to find orders for me to be transferred to a duty station on the East Coast. It was time for me to move to my next duty station anyway, so the timing was perfect.

I was tired of fighting my depression. My romantic relationships had crumbled right before my eyes. I was not present as a mother. I didn't know which way was up. I was making one stupid mistake after another. There I was, a single mother of two children. Not having the best parental examples, I shuddered at the thought of being successful at being their mother. I had to get myself together at least for my children. I could not fail them. They deserved better. Somehow I had to find a way to heal because I had children that did not deserve the broken version of me.

The Marine Corps Air Station at Cherry Point North Carolina was my opportunity to start fresh. That's what I convinced myself to think. Once again, I found my motivation as a Marine to be the best at my job. I thought that if I focused on my boys and my career, I would be fine. I thrust myself into my work. One thing for sure—I knew I was a damn good Marine. Working in a man's world was difficult, but it couldn't be worse than living in the shadow of my father's disappointment, so I strove to become the most outstanding Marine there.

Once again, I got assigned to a unit that put me at a disadvantage—a combat air-wing unit where there were almost 2,000 Marines but only a handful of women. Most of the higher-ups were old school and were stuck in their ways. Word was that they were not happy that we women were being integrated into their unit. Traditionally, this unit had been strictly males, but times were changing fast. Regardless, I was used to being where I wasn't welcome.

My sergeant major gave me a hard time from day one. He was higher ranking than I was, much higher. Being a corporal afforded me some benefits, but mostly, it entailed my being responsible for junior Marines in the office, and I had no issues with my subordinates. I knew how to provide them with incentives so they would respect me and work hard when I needed them to. Since I lived in base housing, I cooked often, and I gave them home-cooked meals as a reward whenever they were working hard or followed the rules.

I was always early to work, so there were many mornings that I was in the office alone. When my sergeant major would walk in, I always respectfully acknowledged him, but he would just stare at me not saying a word. That puzzled me at first, but I would shrug it off and continue with what I was doing. Day after day, he would follow his routine of just staring at me, and that eventually made me so uncomfortable, but I fought the urge to say anything. It is hard for me to articulate just how bizarre it was to have him do that every day, and every time, it was when I was alone. My sensors where ringing—*Danger!*

Several times when he was doing his staring, I asked him if he needed anything, but he wouldn't respond. Just stare. He made sure no one was around whenever he stared at me. It often felt as if he were looking through my clothes. I felt very uneasy. He knew I was uncomfortable with being in the office alone with him, but he would smirk at me and stare as if it gave him pleasure to taunt me that way. Sometimes, I would chuckle due to my nervousness. I mean, what else could I have done? He was much higher in rank than I was, and I had to tread lightly or end up dealing with potential blowback. Women who gossiped about this kind of experience would find their careers spiraling into chaos. I did not plan to be one of them—the casualty of a man projecting his authority. It's not as if I could have just told him to stop staring at me and leave me alone; I had no power, and who would listen to me? All he was doing was staring at me. No big deal, right?

Working in administration presented me with the opportunity to meet and build relationships with many people in different MOSs and of different ranks, and that was a good thing for me. One of these individuals told me to watch my back. Word was that the sergeant major had a thing for me and was "feeling me out". I guessed that meant he wanted to see how I would respond to his aggressive posture. Apparently, he had been talking about me to some senior staff NCOs and had made comments about how he believed I was a waste of a Latina because I messed around with black men and had bastard children with them.

Supposedly, he had said something like, "I'd love to have a piece of that."

I tried hard to stay away from him after being told this. I would wait in my car until I saw my Sergeant get to the office before I would enter the building so the sergeant major wouldn't have an opportunity to hover over me while we were alone. It was exhausting to constantly have to be aware of my surroundings and rearrange my movements in order to feel comfortable. I was already doing that with my regular life and now my work life was disrupted to the point that I did not feel safe there either. *"Keep your head on a swivel Jeanette. Pay attention to your surroundings at all time. Don't trust anyone."* The record played in my head on repeat where ever I went.

One night, I was babysitting the son of a friend from work. His wife Lori (not really her name) came over to pick him up. I was hanging out with two of my Marine friends. They said they would be back; they were going to the store. Lori asked to speak privately as they were walking out the front door. We went into my bedroom, where my son was asleep on my bed next to her son. I led her to the room thinking she was picking up her son. Out of nowhere, she asked me if I was having an affair with her husband.

I nervously laughed and replied, "No!"

I worked with her husband, and we were close, but we were all close. I spent lots of time at their house and mostly with Lori, but I had recently stopped visiting because she was behaving strangely. She would drink a lot and have many different men over to her house while her husband was on training operations away from the base. That had made things awkward for me, so I decided not to hang out with her anymore.

Lori proceeded to ask me about my relationship with her husband. I didn't know how to respond any different than I already had but that was not the answer she was looking for. I wondered what her problem was but then I smelled alcohol on her breath, it reminded me of someone back home. As she spoke, she gently touched my arm as if she were brushing something away. The hairs on the back of my neck stood up. Lori told me that her husband had confided in her that he and I were having an affair. She said she didn't have a problem with it either. Her deal with him was that if she could watch, join in, or have me for herself sometimes, it would be okay with her.

I was offended. Lori touched me more. I attempted to back up and away from her as she continued to grope me and tug at my shorts as if she were trying to pull them off. My heart began to race, and a sense of familiarity came over me. Déjà vu again. A wave of fear washed over me like heat rising within. The children were in the room, so I tried to make as little noise as possible. Eventually I backed up too much, and my legs suddenly buckled. We fell onto the bed with her on top of me. I couldn't even scream.

"What are you doing?" I tried to say, but no words came out. She was smothering me with her breasts as she groped me all over, and I panicked. All I managed to do was whisper, "Please stop!"

I heard the screen door open. My friends were back. Thank God! She abruptly got up and said through gritted teeth, "If you tell anyone, I'll say you were having an affair with my husband and I confronted you. They always believe the wife." Déjà vu again.

Lori left with her son. I was speechless. I couldn't move. One of my friends called out my name, and I snapped back to reality. I left the room trembling; they saw the look on my face, all the color washed from it, and told them what had happened. Both of them said I should report it before Lori. Their concern was that sooner I did the better so I wouldn't look guilty just in case Lori decided to report me anyway.

The next day, I told my sergeant, and he sent me to the one person I dreaded having to go to—the sergeant major. I went into his office and he instructed me to close his door and stand at attention. He was not an officer, and under these circumstances, there was no need to have me do that. We had been briefed regarding proper etiquette when dealing with Marines of the opposite sex; a male military members was not allowed to be behind closed doors with a female of a lower rank. I was already traumatized over what has happened the night before, and then I had to stand at attention as he questioned me. It's normal to be questioned when reporting an incident, but this man was not trying to get information for his report. As he sat at his desk, he asked me questions that I felt were very inappropriate. He didn't even have a pad to write notes.

"So did she caress one breast or both?"
"Did she stick her hands down your pants and feel you down there?"
"Did she kiss you on your mouth and neck?"

The whole time, his face was contorted. Was he being aroused by my recounting the incident? I never really was able to even tell him the whole story because I felt he was more concerned about the sexual details instead of getting relevant information for a full report. So, in order to try to get the *interrogation* over, I told him that she had threatened me with reporting me to my superiors with a made up story.

He replied with, "Okay, thank you for telling me. I'll handle it." Then dismissed me. No one ever followed up and it was as if it never happened.

So again I isolated myself. *Trust no one ...* That became my mantra. I ruminated over the incident and again blamed myself. The truth is, I am the common denominator in all these events, so I figured that I had to be the problem. I had to somehow be attracting these kinds of people, and it was what I deserved. You reap what yo sew. You are what you attract.

* * *

A few months later, I hosted a party at my house for a military member leaving Cherry Point. I took care of my military members, so I was happy to do it. Unfortunately, some people I didn't know showed up and acted recklessly. When alcohol and military members are combined, you never know what you will end up with. I didn't drink since I had the boys there and I did not know everyone personally who were there.

I was in my kitchen getting some food, and a guy I did not know came in. He had a plate of my food in his hand and said it was delicious. In the middle of our short conversation, he said, "Too bad you're a moolie lover!" I didn't know what that meant at the time and as I was about to ask him what it meant, one of my subordinates standing nearby heard his comment and interrupted me.

He walked up to him and asked, "What the fuck did you just say to my corporal?"

That started a fist fight, as hot-headed Marines usually did for less than that. Part of me was grateful that my Marines had stood up for me, but I also hated violence. Whenever I saw fights or physical altercations, my stomach would hurt so bad. Several other Marines jumped in to stop the fight. Eventually, everyone ended up in my front yard screaming and cursing at each other. They were out of control by this point. Not a good thing when you live in base housing either.

Before I had agreed to host this party, I had made it clear to everyone that if there were any problems, I would immediately shut the party down. That was it. Once they were somewhat settled down, I told everyone to go home. There I stood with a mess in my house and everyone gone.

The next day, I learned that my subordinates had gone back to the barracks and had beaten up the Marine who had been disrespectful to me at the party. I was shocked and angry at them. Someone knocked at my door; it was the military police.

They said, "We need to speak to you regarding the incident we have been told happened here last night."

I didn't think there was much for me to tell, so I told them what had happened, and they left.

The nightmare of my military career began the next day. I walked into my office, and once again, my sergeant major was ogling me and smirking. I always acknowledged him by rank out of respect, but he still would never say a word; he would just cross his arms and stare at me creepily. That day, he walked out of the office after his usual intimidation tactics but returned shortly and addressed me.

"I need you to come into my office immediately!" he exclaimed with anger in his voice.

I jumped up from my desk and said, "Yes, Sergeant Major!" and followed him into his office.

I stood at attention and waited; he sat at his desk and stared at me. I did not know what he as waiting for. The room began to spin. I couldn't breathe. Panic gripped me like a vice. Everything seemed to have slowed to a crawl. My mouth was dry. I tried to open it to say something, but nothing would come out. I was getting dizzy and felt as if I were about to faint.

He broke my daze by harshly stating, "I need to hear from you what happened this weekend at your house."

I blinked a few times to get my bearing and told him what had transpired from my perspective. I made it clear that once the fight broke out, I quickly made everyone leave. He asked me if I spoke to my subordinates after they left. I remembered them calling me to ask to come back over, but I told them they could not because they had caused enough problems. Luckily, some other Marines I knew from another unit had come over after everyone had left. They graciously helped me clean up. I gave them the rest of the food and drinks as a sign of my gratitude.

The sergeant major stared at me with judgment and doubt in his eyes. He asked me a few other questions, and while I answered, he intently wrote notes. I didn't think anything of it. I was telling the truth, so I didn't have to worry about anything. So why was my gut telling me something wasn't right?

About a week later, people began to tell me they had been sequestered and interviewed by some investigators regarding the incident. Slowly, distrust and suspicion filled the air wherever I went. Even my junior Marines acted differently toward me in the office. Finally, I was told that I had been accused of and been charged with having gang affiliations, conspiracy to commit assault, lying to a superior, offering sexual favors to subordinates to do my bidding, and a bunch of other charges too crazy for me to recall. I was floored. Was I in an alternate reality? Was this a joke? I had never been in trouble like that in my life. I had always been the epitome of what it meant to be a Marine.

How can this be happening? I always follow the rules. This can't be happening, I thought. *I am so stupid….when will I learn to stop being naive?*

My unit was scheduled to do a two-week war training to prepare for possible deployment. We were sent to Camp Lejeune NC where they had a training site set up to practice combat scenarios. I was excited to finally be doing military combat training instead of being stuck in an office all day. We set up tents to sleep in and bigger tents for us to eat in or have meetings. Depending on our rank, we were responsible for different tasks throughout the training. As a corporal, I was to be on fire watch which meant I would have to be patrolling the camp perimeter. I was given an M-16 and had to walk the perimeter of our camp including the tree line outside our perimeter. I did not mind doing that since I knew Marines would be awake all over the camp and my safety wasn't a real concern. Or was it?

One night while there, as I was patrolling and looking around, I heard noises by the tree line, so I looked in that direction. I didn't see anything at first, so I returned to my duty tent, which was a few yards in the tree line. As I called in my status, I heard branches cracking. I grabbed my rifle and walked outside. Once again, I scanned the tree line and the area around me. Someone stepped from behind a tree. I gasped. It was the sergeant major and of course now he was standing with his arms folded, through the darkness of the night he stared at me like always. My eyes had already adjusted to the darkness so I could clearly see him. He was close enough that I could see his eyes, they were dark from the evil he exuded; they were empty and soulless but piercing and frightening.

My heart was pounding. My eyes darted around to see if there was anyone around. What was he doing? Why was he here? Would anyone hear me if I screamed? I could hear my heart beating in my ears. Instead of letting him see my panic, I acknowledged him loudly using his rank and name. Making sure to hide the fear in my voice as much as possible, then I asked him if he needed anything. He stood there for a moment and then stepped behind the tree and slowly walked away without saying a word. I breathed. I realized I was holding my breath the whole time waiting for his response.

The next day, I was called into the big tent and told that I would be escorted to the main base, where I would be met by two other Marines. I was interrogated by two Naval Criminal Investigative Service (NCIS) personnel at length. It felt as if they were intent on getting me to incriminate myself for some reason. My head was spinning ... My mind was in a fog. I still believed that since I was innocent, I would be okay, so I spoke freely to them. I insisted that the truth would prevail so that they could say and believe whatever they wanted, but eventually they would know the truth and I would be vindicated. Clearly, these two men were not too sure of that. As time went on, I realized that I was in their sights and that they believed I was guilty.

One agent treated me like a criminal and yelled at me trying to force me to sign a so-called confession. When I refused, he screamed that I was being insubordinate and stormed out. The other one played the good cop of the pair. He came at me with fake compassion in his eyes and used a different tactic. He said that he thought I was involved in this big conspiracy but was unaware of it. Absolutely not! I was not that stupid. Was I? There was no way I could have been a part of any of what they were accusing me of even by accident. I was forced to take mug shots and to give my fingerprints. Out of frustration or perhaps because they did not get what they wanted out of me, they dismissed me, and I returned to the training operation at the training camp. When the sergeant major saw me, he looked surprised as if he had not expected me to return.

Once we all returned back to base, things took a turn for the worse. My life became a story one would hear about only in an espionage movie. So many suspicious things would start to happen around me. A friend confirmed that my phones were tapped once I began inquiring regarding weird sounds coming from my phone. Indeed, when I would be on the phone talking to my family or friends, I would hear clicking noises. A Marine driving a light-colored sedan followed me wherever I went. Because I thought I was loosing my mind, one day while at my friends house I checked outside her window and there was the vehicle again. So, I asked her to look outside her window and check if you saw it too. She did on several occasions.

Anyone I befriended was scrutinized and questioned. People stayed away from me more and more until no one came around anymore. I was ostracized and isolated. I felt so alone. I thought I was going crazy. I had no one to turn to. I would go home after work, feed my boys, get them ready for bed and rush into my room just to cry myself to sleep. I hated the world I was living in. What had my life turned into? One weekend, I went home with my boys to visit my family and saw that same vehicle parked outside our building all the way in the Bronx. What the hell did they think I was doing? Who did they think I was?

But I had a guardian angel amid all the chaos. One person who must have felt that I was being mistreated and knew I was wrongfully accused fed me some information. Thankfully, they felt I should be equipped with the truth and provided me a manila envelope filled with positive supportive and corroborating statements from multiple military members. I also discovered that most of the charges brought against me came from that senior staff who was harassing me. The rumor was that he felt slighted at his advances not being reciprocated; people believed he created this outrageous scenario to get back at me.

The investigators had informed me that everyone they had interviewed had made statements stating that I was the mastermind behind everything that had happened in the barracks beginning from my home. Apparently, everything that ensued before and after the incident had all been done at my direction. Fortunately, the documents I received proved the opposite. I cried when I read them all. Of course all tears of happiness and relief. My friends had told the truth, and no one was saying anything negative about me. However, the one person who did say something negative about me was the sergeant major and that

Marine who started the incident at my house. Due to his years of experience and his reputation, they believed what the sergeant major stated so the investigation started due to his involvement.

I had to endure this investigation and everything that came with it for about a year after the incident. I was isolated and alone. My world was collapsing around me. I was being followed and watched. The months of not knowing what would happen next drove me to the brink of insanity. I was on edge all the time, and I startled easily. Most nights, I had nightmares and woke up terrified. I was right back to where I had been in Hawaii. Fear engulfed me at every turn. I felt that people were watching me wherever I went. People were surveilling me as part of the investigation, but paranoia became a part of my daily stress. If anyone glanced my way, I either interpreted it as them judging me or scrutinizing my actions some way, or that they were collecting information to report it back to someone.

* * *

After about a year passed, I received a letter from NCIS. I had been cleared of all charges, but I didn't receive as much as an apology. I know I should have been grateful but after all the accusations, I thought that was the least they could have done. The commanding officer (CO) of my unit was so disgusted with me that he kicked me out of the unit and sent me to the other side of the base with another unit. I still felt shunned. Fortunately for me, the command at my new unit did not tolerate all the shenanigans they heard had gone on and made it clear to others that I better not be mistreated.

Little effort, and too late for me. I had had enough. During the whole investigation, I was selected to be promoted to sergeant. Unfortunately, because I was under investigation, my CO deemed me ineligible to be promoted because my having been involved in a criminal investigation reflected poorly on me as I was not representing myself in the manner suited for a corporal or a sergeant.

Once I was cleared of the charges, I requested mast (It provides a service member the opportunity to communicate not only with his or her immediate Commanding Officer, but also with any superior Commanding Officer in the chain of command up to and including the member's immediate Commanding General.) to the commanding general (CG) of the base and pled my case. I had worked hard and deserved that promotion, and I felt that the least they could do was promote me. Especially since I was cleared of all the charges. Luckily for me, the general listened to my circumstances in an unbiased manner. I was granted a backdated promotion to sergeant once I pled my case enough to give reasonable doubt as to why I should have never been accused in the first place.

During my request mast, I also presented my case regarding the treatment I had received from the powers that be - specifically the sergeant major. I explained how these accusations caused me to have panic attacks and insomnia. I was afraid to go anywhere or have anyone around me fearing having similar situation occur.

I could go nowhere without the sergeant major finding me and playing psychological games with me. He would show up in the most innocuous places—grocery shopping at the commissary, shopping at the base exchange, and even a few times out in town when he would corner me at a store or restaurant. He would just stand and stare at me not saying a word, and I would freeze. Sometimes, I would drop everything I had in my cart and grab my kids and leave.

One incident had me so frazzled that I shook. I was in the commissary with my children. As I turn down one aisle, there he stood at the end arms folded and just staring as usual. I quickly ushered my older son into my cart and turned around so I could go down another aisle, but he popped out at the end of the aisle and just stood there again. I looked around to see if anyone else saw him. Was I losing my mind? Was I imagining this? My breathing would become shallow, and I felt faint. Focusing on my children became my strength.

Just focus on your babies so you can get out of here safely, I told myself so I wouldn't completely lose it there.

I made sure to tell the general about these and a few other incidents. He listened. His face showed that he was contemplating how to respond appropriately and professionally. Then he spoke.

He said, "Just try to stay out his line of sight" and "Avoid him as much as you can."

Every inch of me was vibrating with rage. I'm sure he could see the scowl on my face that read, "are you fucking kidding me? Did you just say what I thought you said?" But instead I stood there silent as he spoke. The general dismissed me believing that I was satisfied with his decision. Actually only partially, but I smiled in agreement. I left the commanding general's office in a panic.

Once I finally mustered the strength and spoke up about all that the sergeant major had been doing, all I received in reply was this. Just as I had feared, once again, my words had fallen on deaf ears. My voice has been ignored and deemed as being inconsequential. Basically, I was being told to suck it up and just deal with it. Find a means to just stay out of his way? My feelings and experience meant absolutely nothing. Who would protect me? I felt all alone again. All I had was my innocent children, and what good was I to them when I couldn't even protect myself? Something had to give. I was a tea kettle bubbling. A thousand tiny bubbles were about to scream.

6

PLAN

Commitment is the spirit of determination and dedication found in Marines. It leads to the highest order of discipline for individuals and units. It is the ingredient that enables constant dedication to Corps and country. It inspires the unrelenting determination to achieve victory in every endeavor. —Marines.com

Discharged

At this point, my whole life was the Marine Corps and my children; nothing was more important to me other than those two things. But, my spirit was broken after all the things I had experienced during those few years prior. I had lost my faith in the system that was supposed to protect people. I exemplified all there was to be a great Marine, but the word of one individual had turned all my hard work into dust. My identity had been stripped away. I was angry and hurt at the Marine Corps and all who had allowed these things to occur. No one stood up for me except for my guardian angel who supplied me with informational ammo to protect myself. I tried to see the silver lining in that, but my list of catastrophes was too long for me to be optimistic about anything else at the time.

Being an administrative clerk gave me the luxury of having access to all the military regulations, rules, policies, and directives. I made it my job to meticulously read, research, and scrub methodically through them all. I wanted out. I was done with the Marine Corps at this point. I felt used and discarded. In my research, I discovered that I could request a discharge based on being a single parent. I submitted my discharge request to my supervisor. Can you believe that when it was sent up to the base general for approval, it was denied? My denial included a response similar to this:

Alternate reality for real! Are they serious? Now I was a great Marine? At that point, I lost my shit. Because I had been having a hard time dealing with the aftermath of all the shenanigans of the past two to three years, I was seeing a therapist and occasionally the base chaplain. They even prescribed me with antidepressants and medication of my panic and anxiety. That day, I went to the chaplain and broke down crying.

After repeating what I had been through, I told him, "I'm so depressed, and I don't want to live this way any longer. If I don't receive the approval to be discharged from the military, I think it will make me want to drive my car straight into the wall of the motor transport compound."

He was taken aback by that; his face showed a glint of genuine concern. He had me stay in his office and wait while he made a few phone calls. After returning to his office, he patiently gave me advice on how to deal with how I was feeling. He gave me validation and asked me to promise I wouldn't hurt myself. He reassured me that he would do all he could to help me. I promised him I wouldn't hurt myself - not completely being truthful. I camouflaged my pain as I returned to work pretending I was fine.

I had their attention at that point; everyone was suddenly listening to what this Sergeant was saying. My supervisor instructed me to resubmit my request soon after my returning to the office. My discharge paperwork miraculously came back a second time, and that time, it had been approved. I had ten days to check out and be discharged.

* * *

Suicide Attempt

I quickly completed all the things needed for my discharge to be processed. I even found a job at a small airport nearby. After finally being discharged from the Marine Corps, I dove into my new job at the airport. I didn't want to think about how much of a failure I felt. This job afforded me the opportunity for a new challenge and distracted me from my horrible life. I needed to get myself together. To have some time to adjust to my new life.

Previously to my being discharged, I took my sons to New York City to stay with my parents for a little while. My mind was spiraling out of control, and I had no idea what I was doing yet again. My parents never noticed me really, so I was able to quietly exist without their seeing my pain. That was when I became an expert at hiding my pain from others.

I worked as much as I could so I didn't have to think about what had happened over the past few years. I was in denial, and I was trying to fill my time with productive things so I wouldn't lose my mind completely. It reminded me of how I survived living back hime pretty much doing the same thing. Whenever things were hard for me at home, I would dive into my school work and excel there. This time it didn't work. At work, I would burst into uncontrollable crying and could not stop.

My job was a solitary one; I worked in the back, putting luggage on or taking it off planes, managing the departures and arrivals of planes, and arranging refueling. It allowed me to practice my poker face. I would cry between flights, wipe my face, and set up what needed to be set up next. This went on for weeks until all at once I was slammed with a ton of uncontrollable emotions—anger, frustration, sadness, bitterness, rage and guilt.

Everything from the past six years just crashed on top of me. I was depressed because I had lost my identity. I was angry because no one who had betrayed me had been held accountable. I was miserable and sad because I had loved being a Marine and thought I would make it my career, but at this point, I had nothing.

I was bitter because I had given up too easily. I was disheartened because I didn't know what I would do next. I was ashamed of myself because I had sent my children to my parents' house because I couldn't deal with anything, including them. Who sends their children into a den of potential abuse? I felt as failure as a mother. I couldn't even think straight enough to protect them. I felt guilty because I hadn't fought harder to tell my story.

My mind played tricks on me too. I'd think, *Did my choices cause this?* and I'd hear, *Yes, you're the reason, and now you have to deal with the consequences of your actions. You're a failure. You deserved all that happened to you. You're just like people said you would be—nothing. Your children are better off without you.* Such thoughts echoed through my head. Sleep never came, so I stared at my ceiling reliving my misery. Crying became my new enemy; each stinging tear resembled a memory sneaking out of my eyes to torture me. Each tear was blood dripping from a wound. I detested the pain I felt. I wanted it to become a faded memory no longer consuming my soul. But how could I end it?

Please, God, make it stop!

I strategized how I could make it all go away. **I would kill myself.** I felt I had no reason to live. How could I face everyone? My children would be ashamed of me if they knew. My family would judge me and blame me for it all. I didn't have anyone on my side. No one was there to support me. I had my medication for anxiety and depression, so my plan was to take it all. In order for it to be more effective, I thought I'd drink liquor with it.

I prepped it all. I sat in my house alone in the dark calculating what I would do next. Everything was laid out in front of me on my coffee table. I would take all my pills and wash them down with liquor. I hoped I would just quietly drift off to sleep and never wake.

I thought, *If this is supposed to happen, I'll be able to do it uninterrupted. So God, if you intend on stopping me, now's the time.*

I was holding onto a glimmer of hope that God would intervene. Obviously, I was conflicted. I filled my hand with some pills from the first bottle and put them in my mouth followed by some juice and a swig of the vodka I had purchased earlier that day from the package store (a store found on military bases that sells liquor at a cheaper price). I filled my hand with the contents of the other bottle and did the same. I mixed some juice with the vodka and drank some of it. I cried the whole time. I sat on my couch thinking about my children. Tears were stinging my eyes and streaming down my cheeks. I loved them so much, but I hated who I had become. I was the worst mother, and they deserved better than what I could give them. The couch felt like it was swallowing me, and I let the feeling engulf me as I felt myself slowly slipping into sleep ...

All I remember next was him coming into my house and tapping at my face saying, "Wake up!" He and his voice seemed distant. I was limp. I closed my eyes again. *Is this real?* I wondered. I just wanted to sleep.

He carried me to the bathroom, and I think I threw up. I guessed he had noticed all the pill bottles and alcohol on my coffee table. He took off my clothes and put me in the shower, and he stepped in with me; he was still fully clothed. The cold water shocked me into consciousness.

The next thing I remember was being in the Carolina East Medical Center in New Bern, North Carolina, for attempted suicide. I spent about two weeks there, time to gain insight into what I had done.

God had answered my prayers. He gave me my reason and the clarity I was seeking. I saw this as a sign. There was something destined for me to do in this world. I needed to decide what I would do with this second chance. Shortly after being released, I moved back to NYC so I could be with my babies. I don't remember much else.

Part II

PROUD MEMORIES

7

EXECUTE

Wrongs in the world do not right themselves. Winning the battles we fight requires an ability to endure more than most and a determination that will not relent in the face of hardships and difficulty. —Marines.com

Depression

When I returned back home from the Marine Corps, I was a completely different person. My family still viewed me as the naive, weak Jeanie they knew. No matter what I did or said they all continued to treat me like the old me. It was so difficult howI still lived in that in between place. Not fully fitting into the civilian world, but no longer belonging to the Marine Corps.

My father's side of the family taunted me and made me the butt of their jokes. "She's just crazy", "Looney looney looney!", "The Marines really messed her up". They walked around me as if I would snap at any moment. My infamous childhood abuser made sure to take advantage of every opportunity she had to make a snide comment towards me. "They really fucked her up just like her damn father".

My mothers side of the family, on the other hand, treated me like if I was broken and fragile. They seemed to be afraid of me and whatI might do.

I suffered with deep depression for a long time. I was swathed in the word as if it were a comforting blanket. I felt relaxed sitting in its dark space of coziness. Being depressed, I knew what to expect, and I had it perfected. Depression never let me down. It was dependable. Strangely enough, depression felt like my only safe place. I could wallow in it and be confident with what it offered. There were no expectations of me there.

Happiness? What was that? Happiness was short lived. Was there a point to happiness? At any moment, someone or something could rip it from under me, so why even try to be happy? Depression and anger were much to be. I could easily keep people away too. Those who tried to stay close would ultimately leave me alone anyway. I could rationalize that away; I knew they would leave even though I was the one who pushed them out.

I walked around with constant sadness to the point that I sometimes felt physically ill. My anger grew in me to where I lashed out in rage at anyone in my way, especially myself. I hid my shame and pain within my anger and rage. You see, I was so intent on making sure to wear the mask of strength. Anger was my version of strength.

If I shared my truth and the pain it accompanied, perhaps others would see just how weak I really was and then I'd be that little girl again. For me, there was no way I could be her again. Jeanie had to go. Jeanie was weak and pathetic. Tears she shed were insignificant and worthless just like she was.

I didn't sleep well most days, and I wanted to sleep when I shouldn't be. Some days, I ate, and other days, I didn't. I didn't feel like doing things others did effortlessly. When I tried to pretend and pushed myself to participate with life, it took all my energy and effort. But it would then lead me collapse from exhaustion afterwards. I couldn't concentrate either, so I overcompensated by filling my mind with external mindless distractions. I would clean or organize incessantly and if I was too physically exhausted to do that, I'd read books or watched television continually.

There were many days I would suddenly be angry for the littlest things. I yelled at my sons for nearly everything because I had little to no patience. One of my sons had mental health and behavioral issues, and his behavior would set me off easily. He didn't deserve the version of his mother he received. Both my sons feared me not knowing whom they would get from one moment to the next. I could see the fear in their eyes when they looked at me and though I wanted to be different I couldn't. My greatest concern was that I was fearful I would do to them what was done to me. Eventually, I became someone I despised when I looked at my reflection in the mirror. Some days, I did not see me; I would see that family member who made sure to remind me what a failure I was and always would be. She haunted my days and nights. Her evil laughter and hateful stare a constant fixture in my mind's eye.

My thoughts were all over the place. Most of the time, I felt worthless because I fixated on my failures and blamed myself for everything that had happened to me. I often thought that God was punishing me for something I had done, and I deserved it all. I martyred myself by believing I had to endure everything happening to me. Sometimes, I even went back to thoughts of how my children would be better off without me. They deserved better than what I was giving them, and I wasn't giving them much.
I couldn't be present, so I pretended and forced myself to do what I thought I needed to for them. Going with the motions, I became a machine. I fed them and provided for them but emotionally I was void. I couldn't even hug them without flinching from the uncomfortable unfamiliar feeling that welled up in me. Affection was foreign to me as I barely received it myself, so sadly, I had no idea how to give it to anyone else.

Strangely enough, I barely remember those days except for the pain and damage I inflicted to those I love, specifically my babies. My greatest fear was that they would remember and hate me and then I would have no one to love me. Somehow I needed to find a way to heal because deep in my soul I knew that my children did not deserve the broken version of me. There was no excuse for me not to make a change when I knew better. Once you know better you do better ...right?

Shame rose in me like lava slowly spewing forced by the gases escaping the magma chamber of a volcano. My shame was a close cousin to my anger. Anger resided somewhere inside of me climaxing at the most inopportune moments bringing out a monster called rage that I was reluctant to release. They both lived in me unfortunately like I was their home, and depression was living in the basement of my soul. Showing its face regularly, to remind me who I was, is anger and guilt and they controlled the house and what was allowed inside. Nothing good was allowed in the proverbial door even though rage and shame often escaped and ran free. Meanwhile, the others left behind kept close guard so I could seem strong.

I transformed into a fragile shell of who I was even more. Depression took over and guided my life like a ship's captain. The worst part was that I became great at faking it, so few people knew of my tormented existence. Most of my family and the few friends I still had were unaware of my struggles.

Every now and then, I let my guard down and would tell someone about my tortured battles. Woefully, I was always disappointed because they would make light of it, use it against me, or just blow me off believing it wasn't possible that I could be dealing with such a dark passenger as I'd describe for them. I suppose I could have been awarded an Oscar; I played the role of having it together so well that not even when I told people about my hurt did they believe me.

Eventually, I slowly began my path of isolation. In my mind, if no one could understand me, what was the point of even putting myself in situations or around individuals destined only to let me down? Sometimes in my depression, I felt lonely as well. Those were the times when I would allow just a hint of my former self to emerge, and I would start a relationship. Regardless of whether it was casual or serious, they were just to momentarily fill the void.

* * *

Most people with depression, PTSD, or anxiety as I had, would self-medicate with drugs or alcohol, but I was afraid of that; there were too many people in my family suffering with drug or alcohol addictions. On the other hand, I was no better than them, as these relationships were my drug of choice. I chose dysfunctional relationships because I knew that they would crumble sooner or later. Later, I realized I was doing this on a subconscious level.

I pursued men who were unavailable to me, and not unavailable necessarily because they were involved with other women. They were unavailable due to their chasing their careers, being more concerned with their own needs, multiple women, or some other vice. Deep down I think I knew they would never be able to handle the ugliness of who I really was. Worst of all, instead of my continuing to focus on myself and what I needed and deserved so I could be the best mother to my children, I somehow found the most broken men out there and decided to make them my project as a replacement for my own healing.

They used me too. I know, I know, twisted mindset - absolutely. Dysfunctional as it sounds, I thought I was doing something righteous and getting something out of it for myself. Obviously, they would never commit to me or even put me first. Every one of these relationships was doomed to fail from the start.

Admittedly, in these moments though, I felt passionate, intense emotions toward them, probably on the level of intensity as when someone uses drugs. They gave me a momentary high of some kind. The brief attention they gave me or when they showered me with compliments like "You're the best woman I've ever met", "You're fine as hell", or "You are mine". Comments as simple as these and more, gave me brief satisfaction and gratification and I fell for them. Oddly enough, most of the time I knew they were lying yet I believed them. Well, I wanted to believe them, so I let myself. As intense as they made me feel, all of it would forcefully collide with the truth I feared but knew.

An oxymoron for sure. Once I decided to see through their lies and confront them, the way they treated me changed abruptly to aloofness, and my depression would peek its ugly head out. Those were times when I no longer controlled my feelings and I would emotionally collapse and spiral into a deeper and darker place. In my mind is where I fought to keep myself from completely going insane. Once again, I would end up in the space of wanting to end it all. I would blame others when in reality I had put myself where I was. The only thing that kept me from slipping was looking at the faces of my beautiful sons; they gave me strength.

Momentarily the clouds and haze would clear, and I had moments of clarity. Then, I would ruminate on why the hell I had let some man make me feel insignificant and worthless. It was as if I had no self-worth or self-respect. The more I allowed myself to experience these unnecessary, futile, and fleeting affairs, the clearer it became to me that I was overcompensating for the pain I had not admitted to or addressed. Jeanette things needed to change.

Anxiety, Panic Attacks, and Nightmares

Eventually, anxiety became my best friend. It snuck up on me like fog rolling into the harbor. Anxiety became my other companion and a reminder to all my failures. My days began with excessive thoughts or fears and uneasiness for ordinary situations to the point where I would work myself up and either throw up or nearly poop myself.

Most days, I walked around with chest pains and heart palpitations or feeling dizzy and suddenly sweating profusely. I despised what I had become more and more every day. I barely slept because I would have vivid dreams of being on the beach and him on top of me. I smelled the salt air and the breeze coming off the ocean. I felt myself sinking into the sand like quicksand and it wanted to swallow me or wrap me in its arms made of finely crushed microscopic rock. I would wake up jumping out of my skin.

I could no longer distinguish between what I dreamt being part of a nightmare or flashes of real memories from that night. I hated the beach and especially sand. If I smelled suntan lotion, I immediately felt guarded and sick to my stomach. Avoidance of anything that resembled the beach became a chore for me.

My panic attacks were the worst. I feared everything. My heart would race uncontrollably, and I would have sudden urges to flee even when I knew there was no reason for me to feel that way. Some days, I found myself avoiding going to the grocery store for fear that people would see right through me and know I was damaged. Looking down a grocery isle, as I shopped, made my heart race because I expected the sergeant major to pop out suddenly to torment me. Obviously, I knew he would never be there, but the feeling was real for me and that over-shadowed commonsense. So, I would be consumed with the sudden urge to flee the store.

My tortured soul was in constant turmoil. A part of me desired to be out in the world experiencing and enjoying life, but the unyielding pull from my apprehension was stronger; it overwhelmed me and controlled everything I did. When I mustered the energy to venture out, I was always on alert looking over my shoulder and paying particular atten-tion to anyone who glanced at me. My paranoia made me sit with my back to the wall or make sure to face the doorway so I could see every-one who entered. My senses we always on alert anticipating something horrible about to happen. It was so exhausting that I ventured outside less and less.

All of this affected my ability to parent my sons effectively. I did not know what I was doing or how I would continue this way. Both of them deserved a mother better than the one they were cursed with. I searched for any way to gain insight into how to be a better mother. Because I was ashamed to tell anyone at first, I used television shows to guide me through behaving like a functioning parent. Shows like *The Cosby Show*, *Full House*, *Growing Pains*, *Home Improvement*, and *Who's the Boss* became my guides to parenting. Seeing the love and compassion these fictitious families shared inspired me to do the same. I had no one else to turn to. If I told others, they would say that I was crazy or that something was seriously wrong with me and I needed to get myself together. My family was no place to turn to. Hiding my secret was my other job. Even if I was using fictional families as my reference, at least I was trying something better than what I knew.

The only thing I had control of was what I taught myself, so I also read a lot of how-to books on parenting and self-improvement. Since I didn't have the best examples of what a parent should be, I decided to read about what it took to be a good parent.

One of the last books I read was *What Happened to You?* by Dr. Bruce D. Perry. It made me realize that what had happened to me as a child influenced how I behaved as an adult. My traumatic experiences had impacted me and rewired my brain. I learned that my repetitive exposure to stressors lowered my stress response therefore giving me a predisposition for the development of mental and physical health aliments. I had to break the patterns and change my mindset.

I was surprised to learn that those whose minds focus on the negative things which have happened to them, will move in a negative direction in life. I was determined to make a positive change and not allow the truth of my past to overshadow the good things currently in my life. I would no longer put the focus on the terrors in my mind. The beginning of my attempt to break the curse.

I also found parenting classes to attend. I moved a lot so wherever I was, I connected with my local resources so that I could find a community center, mental health clinic or any non-profit organizations that offered classes. Somebody out there had the answers for me. It just had to be true. If I wanted to become the best mother for my boys, I needed to do whatever I could. Truth be told, logically I was not the only women as a single parent trying to maneuver within this thing called life. Once you know you are doing wrong, you must find out how to do right. So, my quest began.

* * *

It's not fun living with anxiety, depression, and panic attacks. I grew up believing in God, but the devil disguised himself in the form of these negative thinking patterns and destructive behaviors so I could not think clearly enough to ask God to help me. A big part of me was still punishing myself. I was somehow stuck in the belief that I had deserved everything that had happened and was continuing to happen to me. There were nights where I would ask God, *Why me?* There were nights I would share all my fears and worries with God. Regrettably, the darkness and wretchedness in me prevented me from hearing His reply. The answers may have been there, but I was blinded by the darkness of depression, anxiety, and anger so I could not see nor hear Him tell me.

It took many years of needless suffering for me to get to a place where I just had had enough and realized that I could ask for help from those who were educated in mental health. Coming from a traditional Latino/Hispanic background, I was taught that your business was private, and psychologists and psychiatrists were quacks, so I struggled with that as well.

I was blessed to come across some very helpful people who provided me with the resources I needed to get the help I desperately needed. Without judgment, they listened to my problems and gave me their options. I was skeptical at first, but they were speaking from a perspective of positive results themselves as they had suffered some of the same things I did.

Over the past twenty-five-plus years, I have experienced frequent nightmares, many repetitive and tormentingly recurring, and I still occasionally have these nightmares. I am not saying that everything has gone away or that it absolutely will. The difference for me now is that I don't ruminate over my nightmares as I had in the past.

I have experienced a flood of horrific, suppressed memories progressively coming back to me throughout the years as well. I have had to learn to deal with them and sometimes process them with the help of my therapist or psychiatrist. One thing I have learned about the intense emotions accompanying these nightmares is that I would end up depressed, startle easily, and experience increased anxiety and fleeting moments of suicidal ideations. It taught me that even though I have these feelings, I can give them validation and release them so they no longer have a hold of me.

Thankfully, my path of healing has allowed me to move past the intense emotions and memories and be okay. My days will not be ruined, and I don't obsess over my nightmares or the emotions they conjure up. I have learned to transform my pain into power. Unfortunately, there are still times where I have these nightmares, but I am unaware of them; I only know that they happened because my husband would often tell me in the morning. According to his accounts, I wake him with my cries sometimes.

Ultimately, what I want people to take away from this book is that healing after trauma is work. It does get better, but sometimes, a sound, smell, or some other external stimulus will trigger your memory and you may have a negative response. My anxiety and panic attacks still happen every now and then, but they do not control me to the point that I cannot interact with people. My emotions no longer hold me hostage.

I recall times I have gone to the beach and suddenly felt uneasy and frozen in fear. The smell of the ocean and the sand make me feel ill, and I cannot remain there, so I have to leave, but having the tools to deal with those moments encourages me, and I no longer fear total meltdown. When I have these sudden memories or triggered flashes, I can process them and remove myself from the environment and regain my composure. I allow myself to have those feelings without judgment or criticism. I acknowledge what I felt, feel the emotion, process how it made me feel, and then let it go.

8

COORDINATE

In our world, in ourselves, and in our way, there are conflicts, challenges, and obstacles that must be fought confidently and defeated convincingly for our Nation to prevail. These looming battles come in many forms and occur on many fronts, but each comes down to a critical choice: to demand victory or accept defeat. To pull together or fall apart. To give in or cave in. —Marines.com

New Belief System

To find the right path, I had to get the help that worked best for me mentally, physically, and spiritually. We've all heard that we should be careful about what we ask for. Well, I was in a period of my life where I was deeply and wholeheartedly seeking for my soul to be cleansed. My relationship with God became stronger than ever, but I still struggled with finding peace and happiness in the most important aspects of my life.

So, I prayed. I asked God to bring me those things I needed and those people He knew I needed the most. I had to put myself in situations I was not comfortable with too. You see, when you ask for God's help, you cannot sit at home and think it will come to you on a silver platter out of nowhere. No one is going to come up to your door and know to then say, "here Jeanette, I have your solution to all your problems". Life doesn't work that way.

One day at church, the pastor was preaching about faith and taking action. It blew my mind how this message ringed as if it was made specifically for me. The scripture given to us to read was: "But someone will say, 'You have faith; I have deeds.' Show me your faith without deeds, and I will show you my faith by what I do" (NIV James 2:18–19). I understood this to mean that if you are living in faith in Christ, the result will be believers contributing in good works in their lives as well as others'. Those who don't do this have a metaphorically dead faith.

Then perhaps ultimately it means what we do should be the direct reflection of what we believe. Simply declaring faith in Christ is pointless because you should be doing something to represent your faith through some sort of action. In essence, people who believe in something act on what they claim to believe in. If someone claims to have faith but it doesn't cause him or her to act on it, it isn't faith; it is fraudulent or just talk. So, since I believed in what God promised me, I had to act, find the knowledge, and use it to become a better me as a child of God.

Those who do not believe in God can still use this as a basic principle in life. Read that scripture and see for yourself. You cannot say you want things to change if you are not taking an active role in making any changes in your life.

* * *

I knew then that I had to act to find peace. Soon after, I went to the Veterans Administration Hospital near me, and I was given the clarity I needed. For many years, I had been in individual therapy yet I had resisted any form of group therapy. I thought being in the same space as others who experienced what I had would be too overwhelming, but God gave me the strength to take the next step in my healing. I signed up for a group class for women dealing with PTSD brought on because of MST. I was assigned a very intelligent young woman named Dr. Jimenez; she became my therapist and she was assigned to work with me and my goals.

Initially I was resistant to having a new therapist to have to start the process all over again. Telling my story and explaining all the things that I struggled with throughout the years, was not something I looked forward to. Could I trust her, would she be able to provide me with the insight to the next stage of my healing? I prayed for clarity in my heart, mind and in my spirit. The more I visited with her, the clearer it became. She was honestly invested in my healing. At that point, I believed I received the clarity on what I needed to do next. I had been through all kinds of individual therapy and treatments through the years, but I felt a strong desire to find something new. Medication was not my ultimate goal right now, but that is not to say that medication is ineffective.

Years ago, I needed medication desperately, and I tried so many different ones. It was hard trying over and over. There were times that I didn't want to take another pill because of the way some of the medications made me feel, until my doctors and I found the right combination that worked for me. I won't provide a list of what they were because they aren't important to my story, but I will share with you just how important it is for some. For the first time in my life I was struggling with a chemical imbalance that affected how I functioned daily and how I processed situations. Medication helped calm things down for me so that I could have a clear mind in order to work on my mental healing.

Every person has his or her own path; what worked for me does not necessarily mean it will work for you. However, you must understand that you need to work closely with your psychiatrist and health care provider to find the right combination of medications that will help you in your situation. Some people may not even need medication, and that too is okay.

My goals included finding balance. I wanted to find peace, joy, and happiness again, and I would do the hard work required for that, whatever it may be. It was challenging at first, and my mind played tricks on me often. Dr. Jimenez was firm but kind, thankfully. She called me out on my bull and pushed me in ways I needed to be pushed. Her approach was different; she focused on the whole body working together to heal the mind, and she opened my mind to new possibilities. I learned so much from her and the classes she led and in our individual therapy sessions.

One methodology she presented was the holistic approach to healing. I learned about the mind, body, and soul connection and how they relate to each other. Our mental, physical, and spiritual parts are interconnected and work synergistically—each affects the others, so when one is out of balance, it will affect the others.

Mind

Using the information mentioned above, I had to create a new belief system for myself. I had to change the way my mind focused on certain things. Growing up in my family taught me to focus on the negative and not really have solutions to make a change that could positively make a difference about my circumstance. With this system I learned to make conscious choices to work at keeping stress, chaos, and worry to a minimum. Wherever I had control, I needed to eliminate unnecessary stress. Honestly, my stressors were mainly work, some family members, and how I responded to other external situations that I had no control over but ruminated on. All of these had to change for me to heal.

Your life moves in the direction of your dominant thoughts, so whatever you set your mind and focus on is what your life and emotions will become. You are a reflection of what you put your energy into. Every day, I had to be mentally present so I could be able to purposefully choose positive thoughts and gratitude for my blessings. I was determined to find the joy in the little things.

I understood that whatever I allowed my mind to focus on—positive or negative—manifested in my life. I learned that I actually had power over my mind in ways I had not even fathomed. Daily practicing made it easier for me to see the fruits of my labor too. The more I used my mind to regulate my emotions, the more I was able to concentrate and find peace. All the pieces began to come together, and I had physical concrete proof coming into fruition whenever I made the effort. It's not selfish to love yourself. When you make happiness a priority by taking care of yourself first, it actually is an unselfish way of showing those you love just how much they mean to you. Being the best version of who you are is what you manifest when you practice this.

When negative thoughts creep up on me, using this method, I no longer work at ignoring them or pretending they don't exist. Instead, I acknowledge them, thank my mind for telling me, and ask myself if it was a thought that was true or useful to me right now. Once I decide that a negative thought is no longer useful, I release it. My thought distortions are clarified and transformed. I am able to sleep better too. I still don't sleep eight to nine hours at once, but I can say that I now have three to four hours of restful sleep whereas previously I would wake up nearly every forty-five minutes to an hour during the night.

Body

What most of us do not realize is that our bodies remember things too. I am not necessarily talking about remembering from the perspective of psychological memories. What is meant by this concept is that when you stuff your emotions deep inside, when you ignore your pain, when you don't speak up about how you feel or the negative things you have experienced and instead smile through the pain, your body remembers and keeps score. The National Library of Medicine (NIH) states, "MST is also connected to an increase in medical illness, mainly pain-related symptoms involving multiple organ systems, including gastrointestinal, neurological, genitourinary and musculoskeletal." (https://pubmed.ncbi.nlm.nih.gov/24006322/ I am a living and true testament to that. Things began to manifest in me slowly, but I ignored all the signs. Being a single mom did not allow me the opportunity to break down or be in pain to the point that I could not function. So, I ignored my feelings. I pretended that everything was ok when it really was not.

I ignored my physical pain too. It started with unknown pain and uncontrollable headaches coupled with bouts of memory issues. Then years later, I started having gastrointestinal issues, acid reflux, and back pain. Sometimes, I addressed my issues, but when the doctors didn't have answers or just wanted to throw medications at me, I stopped mentioning things unless they made me unable to perform at work or at home. The fear of not being heard crept up again, and I would shut down.

In my forties, I started having a lot of medical problems that did not seem to have any connection to one another. Nothing made sense to me or the doctors. I thought I was becoming a hypochondriac. One day, I would have an asthma attack, and then I would have an allergic reaction to things I had not previously reacted to. Suddenly I would be bed ridden and unable to walk for days, then I would have excruciating stomach pains with no real cause.

In the middle of the night, I would have episodes of jumping out of my sleep feeling like I was falling—a lot—only to discover that my breathing was stopping while I slept. Later, I was diagnosed with sleep apnea. I began to gain a lot of weight from all the medications I was given, and my pain grew worse. My feet started to swell and ache to the point that it prevented me from walking as I used to. My memory seriously started being affected to the point that it prevented me from doing my job the way I was accustomed to. My back issues got worse, and some days, I could not walk at all – even sitting hurt.

In 2018, I was diagnosed with lupus, and I really struggled with that diagnosis. On the one hand, I was relieved to learn that all my ailments were real and that there was a name for what I suffered from, but on the other hand, I was disappointed in myself because the core of me knew that I had allowed the pain of all my traumas to envelope me to the point that it affected my health since I had refused to address and release them. Eventually, I understood that my body was reacting to what my mind was holding onto. I could not have a healthy body that could take care of me if I was not taking care of the other two parts of who I was as a whole. I needed to find the balance in them all.

I had to start eating in a healthy manner. So, I researched and dis-covered the foods that best fed my body and nourished me. Eating for pleasure had to be at a minimum. There were foods that I was allergic to as well, so I eliminated them from my diet. I incorporated more fruits and vegetables into my diet, and I had to make sure to drink plenty of water daily.

Physical activity had to be implemented into my daily routine so that it became an important part of my wellbeing. Because I struggled to walk and was regularly in pain, I had to find a form of physical activity that would work for me. Walking slowly and stretching became my activity until I could move on to more-intense forms of exercise. I had to remind myself that I was no longer physically capable of engaging in activities I used to, so I had to take it slowly. I learned to be kind to myself. It wasn't easy either.

Swimming is good as well. You can exercise your whole body without fear of compression to your back and knees. The advantage of developing regular physical activity habits and eating right will be noticeable in so many aspects of your life. You will generally feel better, have more energy, and essentially have an easier time feeling emotionally well.

When we exercise, our bodies release chemicals called endorphins, which work with the receptors in our brain and lower our perception of pain. These endorphins also trigger a positive feeling in your body. I saw that my whole demeanor changed when I followed a regular exercise routine and made sure to get regular rest.

Soul

The soul is one of the most important parts to having a balanced and complete you. It took me a long time to put the pieces together and be able to strengthen this part of my being. I had grown up in the Catholic Church, but as I grew into adulthood, I desired more. No offense to Catholics, but the ceremonial drab church services left me yearning for something deeper. Sadly, in my experience, I did not receive the connection I desired when I attended church.

My first experience with a nondenominational Christian church opened my soul to something much more profound for me. I learned that I could have a serious, personal relationship with God. I learned that I could speak to Him and tell Him all my dreams and fears. It makes me sad that never learned this sooner. Some of you may not believe in the same thing, but I think we all believe there is something greater than ourselves. I hope. Call it the universe, the divine being, or spirituality; whatever you believe can still be integrated in the mind, body, and soul concept.

We can be in touch with our souls in many ways. For me, it was going to church, praying, and following a basic doctrine centered on what the Bible taught. Having a church family was important to me as well; that made me feel a part of something greater than myself. Those who do not believe in God can find a greater purpose through perhaps volunteering or some type of activism in their communities.

Being compassionate with ourselves and others is another way to connect with our souls, and we can do that through yoga, meditation, connecting with nature, and wanting to live lives of service to others. When we do selfless things for others, we focus less on what we lack, and that can give us peace, joy, and lives characterized by love.

9

MANAGE

"To protect our Nation's ideals, America turns to its Always Faithful. Those who share an uncommon bond for a common cause. Who fight until they win in the battles not everyone can fight? For the promises that America has made. For the promise that America is. Marines remain true to our motto of Semper Fidelis – 'Always Faithful.'" Marines.com

Ask for Help

Asking for help is not a weakness. Seeking help should never make us feel like failures. To heal from any trauma, we have to ask for help and allow others to give it to us. Asking and receiving help were two of the hardest things for me. When you grow up in a family in which there are secrets, dishonesty, mistrust and betrayal all the time, you don't naturally have the wherewithal to know how to ask for help or to trust anyone will give it to you without conditions. Instead, you learn to keep things to yourself and conceal your truth. Therefore, perpetuating the secrets and lies.

I was taught that you don't tell others outside of the immediate family about your problems. I grew up constantly being told that I needed to be always strong and that I couldn't trust anyone. I know—confusing, right? So, I wasn't supposed to cry when my feelings were hurt or even tell anyone I was hurt; I had to grin and bear it. Then I joined the military, where that concept was reinforced even more. Well, I have to tell anyone who also believes this, those beliefs are all lies.

Fortunately for me, I was blessed to meet awesome people along the way to my healing. These individuals were like my angels on earth. Though apprehensive at first, they showed me that I could trust, I could tell them some of my deepest secrets without using it against me. I couldn't recognize it at the time, but they gave me little nuggets of information which ultimately opened my eyes to what healthy adulthood was supposed to look like. Little by little, I took those nuggets and implemented them into my life.

* * *

If you are veteran, the Veterans Administration (VA) has a lot of programs suited to help in numerous areas where someone may need it. They also have resources extend into your local community. Just a year or so after being honorably discharged from the Marine Corps, I met two Viet Nam veterans who were volunteers and service officers with the Veterans of Foreign Wars. My father attended Vietnam Veterans group meetings since I was a little girl myself and I remember going with him to these meetings sometimes. These two gentlemen knew him from those meetings as well. I felt comfortable talking to them as they were father figures and being veterans made them more credible. They took me in and guided me through the VA system and how to get the help I needed. If you are a veteran, you quickly learn just how difficult it is to maneuver the VA system and all the benefits available to us veterans. The biggest issue is that a lot of available access and benefits are not displayed or listed in their entirety; so, unless you ask someone directly then you won't be told. I would call it a "if you don't ask, they won't tell" type of system. Anyway, initially, I was over-whelmed because I didn't think I was mentally ready to receive the help I desperately needed, but I did take mental notes. I took what I needed at the time and tucked away the nuggets of knowledge they gave me for future reference.

* * *

I struggled during the last ten years of therapy. My mind played tricks on me, and I could not come to terms with asking someone to help me with my problems. I mean, I thought that was stupid. They were my problems, and how in the heck would talking about them help me? I thought that hashing out past experiences and digging into my memories so I could remember things I suppressed would only hurt me. Often, I would start therapy or a treatment, but then in the middle of it, I would give up, make excuses and stop showing up to my appoint-ments. Some of my therapists would eventually just remove me from their care. In most of these incidences, I thought that I knew better. In my mind, what they were saying was a waste of my time, or the treatment brought up pain I was not ready to address. If that happens to you, it's okay. We all get the help we need when we are ready to receive it. The important thing is that we learn how to ask for help.

I want to acknowledge the therapists, social workers, and psychiatrists who attempted to help me through the years. Though I quit and moved on, I eventually found where I needed to be and developed the space and mindset to be receptive to the help I desired and needed. Everything they tried to teach me during the years did not fall on deaf ears; later on, everything ended up making sense, and I implemented the tools they gave me in my healing.

Years later, I sought help again. The Vet Center—Readjustment Counseling Center was one of the first places I went to where I gave in to the process completely. Here you will find fellow veterans who have suffered from similar issues. Those same individuals are the social workers and therapists who help their fellow veterans. They too asked for help and got it. Afterward, they pursued their degrees and gave back by working with and for their fellow veterans. I received a lot from the Vet Center. I met some of the best therapist there. The best part of going to a Vet Center is that you don't necessarily have to go there to see a therapist. Often you can find groups of veterans meeting and just hanging out. It feels like home in those offices. You can also gain access to lists of your local community resources. Not only is there help for women who suffer with MST but also, combat veterans and their families.

Finding the Right Help

What works for me might not work for you. I had to go through a lot before finding the right help for me. I didn't follow trends or do what everyone else thought was best for me; I had to dig deep and be my own advocate. I did my due diligence and researched different therapies including medication. I was resistant to medication because I believed it just numbed the pain; I was doing that on my own, so I thought that medication would not help me.

Thankfully, I was assigned a therapist who helped me reconcile with the idea of medication helping me. She showed me that medication was not the be all and end all. Sometimes, we can use medication as a tool to help balance our systems. Our system is battling because of all the chemicals our bodies release when we are in the fight-or-flight state. Those suffering from PTSD, depression, anxiety, and panic disorder as I was may need to get their systems back in order or in sync, and medication can facilitate that.

I found medication to be useful when I coupled it with talk therapy. There are many forms of talk therapy, and just as with medications, you need to find the kind that works for you. I used several kinds that were very helpful.

Cognitive therapy is a form of psychotherapy that teaches us that the way we think about things affects how we feel emotionally. The main goal of cognitive therapy is to educate us on a straightforward concept —We cannot control every aspect of the world around us, but we can take control of how we construe and deal with our environment.

I had to learn patterns of problematic thinking using cognitive processing therapy (CPT), and cognitive behavioral therapy (CBT) is a form of CPT. CPT is a specific type of cognitive behavioral therapy that helps a person learn how to alter and contest unhelpful beliefs related to the trauma previously faced. This type of therapy was developed by Patricia Resick, PhD, to help treat those with PTSD.

For me, CBT worked the best. It allowed me to slowly take steps toward changing the behaviors that kept me stuck in misery. Since I had several issues to tackle, I focused on one at a time. It was very useful because this method didn't make me feel stressed. It allowed me to practice the methods, and if I felt overwhelmed, I could pause. I still practice these techniques even now.

Positive Coping Methods

After my traumatic experiences in the military and the struggles with trying to deal with the aftermath of military sexual trauma, I lost who I was. Unbeknown to me, I had suppressed many of those memories so I could function, but my body kept track of my pain. I camouflaged all my pain by working hard to do other things to the level of compulsive obsession. That was not the answer.

At first, I went to school and tried to get as many degrees as I could. I earned a diploma in network engineering and data communications, and I earned an Associates' degree in digital arts and animation and a Bachelor of Arts in multimedia arts and design. All of these I completed with small breaks in between and amid dealing with the challenges of being a single parent and my mental health problems. I spent so much time going to school that I yearned to be back in school as soon as I was done. I believe that the accomplishments and accolades I received by earning these degrees feed my desire to be "special" or "smart" in my family's eyes.

I read—a lot. Books became a way to escape into a story so I wouldn't have to deal with the realities of my life. At first, I read mostly mystery and fantasy books, and then I moved on to self-help books.

I would keep my house so tidy and orderly to the extent that I tortured my children into being a part of my obsession. I would force them to clean their rooms and clean them again if how they had cleaned was not up to my standards. I clearly remember one incident where I had instructed my boys to clean their rooms. Only eight and nine years old at the time, the demands of an obsessive mother in manic mode must have been so traumatic for them. After telling them to clean their rooms, with no real instruction or assistance, I would go in their room and dismantle it.

My rage would throw me into a yelling fit where I would scream at them and tell them how disappointed I was in their failure to do what I told them to do. Everything that they cleaned up or made an effort to put away, I dumped in the middle of their room and would scream, "now do it again!"

What an absolutely horrible mother! What the hell was wrong with me? I sound just like my childhood abuser, I was turning into her and that was my worst fear. The generational toxic curse had to be broken. Every time I would behave this way towards them, shortly afterwards I would reflect on my behavior and cry. All the emotions that I felt in my childhood came rushing back and reminding me that I prayed for God to make sure I would never behave this way with my own children but here I was. I knew better but I wasn't doing better. My poor babies did not deserve to e treated this way.

I became depressed, bitter, and angry, and I isolated myself often and became void of emotion. All that I desired no longer mattered. The idea that things would get better for me was a distant memory. I lived in a hole of despair and misery with no hope of digging myself out of it.

I would search to fill the void with dysfunctional relationships, investing in them to the point they became my job. Somehow, I believed that if I convinced others to love me, I would be fine, and perhaps the darkness would fade away. All I had to do was get someone to love me so I could feel better. I lied to myself repeatedly and allowed others to treat me in ways I would never want a man to treat my daughters. Sadly, at the time, I didn't know any better.

Growing up, I saw my father mistreat the women in his life. Yeah, he was a provider, but he had many other women and they seemed to know about each other. He had a gift of manipulation and smooth-talking skills like a salesman. Sometimes these women would even physically fight over him. All of these women were driven to do things that was probably out of character for them. Now that I had experienced similar toxic relationships, I came to better understand how easy it is to fall in love with the idea of someone who you believe loves you. I wanted to break the cycle.

The first thing I needed to do was accept who I was. I had to come to a place of loving the me I had become—good and bad. My healing had to start in me, not outside of me. Using and searching for love from another individual was definitely not the answer. One day, I woke up and made a conscious decision to choose myself. Instead of trying to fix others, I looked at myself and the areas I needed to work on. This decision required me to do some soul searching, setting boundaries and setting the path to fixing myself. The days of being used and taken advantage of were gone. No more! I chose me.

Hope showed its face and reminded me I was stronger than I believed, but that wasn't enough for me. It was always short lived, and I fell short of living up to my full potential. One day, I looked into the eyes of my beautiful children and saw that spark in them that I longed for. I prayed that I would not extinguish it in them. My spark was gone, but I had no right to repeat the patterns I knew were toxic and ruin them in the process. When I recognized that, I gained the strength to seek a way out. I knew I had to cope with what had put me where I was and ultimately heal my pain. Yes, I came from dysfunction, but I could no longer use that as an excuse and repeat the cycle in another generation. Knowledge is power, and I knew better, so I had to do better. God made me the steward of these souls, so it was my responsibility to raise them the right way.

* * *

Positive coping methods can ultimately provide those who have survived sexual trauma with an outlet to redirect their focus. If there is one technique, that has worked the best for me, I would have to say it is when I focused on positivity. We don't realize how important it is to change our mindsets to being more positive on the inside and how we respond to external things. I believe we all have control of our destinies;

we can control what is determined by the actions we take today. We can develop a positive mindset and grow spiritually when we decide to not allow the bad energy of the things around us to affect us negatively. We can master letting go instead of receiving negativity, absorbing it and allowing it to rattle our spirits.

Unfortunately, I grew up in an environment where the focus was always on something negative. The adults around me constantly spoke about one horrific instance of something or another. I could come home with a report card with grades in the 80s and 90s, but instead of my parents praising me for the effort, I was chastised and scolded for not trying harder and earning 100s. Many times, when I would get a new dress, I would be excited to show it off, but my happiness was quickly squashed.

"You're too skinny and tall. That dress doesn't fit right. It looks ridiculous on you."

I would rush home from school with an award for a project, but the response I would receive was, "Anyone could have done that. Maybe you should focus on math more."

We need to be mindful of how we respond to our children because how we do that can leave lifelong scars in their souls. Even if you have one parent who praised you as I did, having other family members consistently belittling and making you feel like a failure will be the memory that stands out. As humans, unfortunately, we are more inclined to remember the negative. Perhaps it's because of the sting.

Positive coping enables us to see the glass as half full instead of half empty. We can enjoy the view and be more present. Positivity also helps with the other techniques in healing therapies. We need to find ways to develop positive mindsets in order to have a possibility of overcoming trauma. Perhaps positivity can be considered the facilitator and motivator of our healing.

I definitely can attest to its effectiveness too. I use this method daily. If a difficult situation arises, I am purposeful in looking for the positive in the outcome, so I do not obsess over the negative possibilities.

Something in me keeps telling me that if I focus on the negative, it will produce a negative outcome. So just as they tell us in church to ask God for what we want, we have to sit in a positive space if we want to see positive results.

Another positive coping method for me is my artwork. I found a space in my home where I can comfortably work in peace. My art room is where I read, meditate, draw, paint, and write. Some days, I just listen to music in my comfortable chair. In the past, I used to allow myself to get sucked into the misery of my darkness and would sit in a room with the curtains drawn and the lights off. Now that I have identified my triggers and what works for me, I make sure that my space is bright and filled with positive images and quotes.

Some of you might not have a space like mine, but you can find what works for you. Perhaps you can sit on your back porch, go to a coffee shop and sit quietly in a corner, go to a library and perch yourself somewhere that makes you feel safe and comfortable, or go to a park and watch people walking by or children playing. The trick is to discover your positive space.

10

ASSESS

Marines must have the unwavering grit to continue on when others quit. To fight through anything—with everything.
—Marines.com

New Outlook on Life

Once I realized that my pain was affecting my children and those who genuinely cared about me, I realized that I had to figure out how to change my view of my life so I could move forward in a positive way. I decided to develop a new outlook on life and take the steps necessary to do something different. Everything I had done before now had not worked, so obviously, I needed to do something different to change. The definition of insanity is repeating the same thing while expecting a different result. This clarity opened my eyes so I could stop behaving in an insane manner.

Instead of staying fixated on being a victim or living the life of a broken individual, I shifted my attention to what I had control of. I could not change the past or what those who had hurt me had done, but I could change how I moved forward. My energy was better used making me the best version of myself I could be. I decided I wanted to be a better mother, sister, daughter, friend, and eventually wife.

Another way I stayed on the path to my redemption was by using the techniques I kept in my toolbox. Okay, I don't really have an actual toolbox; I mean that I regularly used the techniques that worked the best for me. Due to my memory issues, I wrote messages to myself on stickie notes, my phone's notes app or I carried a small notebook so I could write things down that inspired me or gave me the positive energy I needed.

Identifying the thought patterns that served me poorly was one technique I saved in my toolbox. I had this record that played in my head telling me that my assault had been my fault and that I should have known better. That had me in a perpetual state of guilt and shame, but once I identified this distorted thought pattern, I realized how it negatively affected my emotions. Every thought and feeling you are having right now is manifesting your experience for your future. Therefore, if you don't like how your life is looking, change it. Stop looking back; let go and move forward.

Once I made these connections, I applied another technique. My distorted thought patterns were negatively affecting how I felt about myself. Cognitive distortions are the predispositions or patterns of thinking or believing that are false or inaccurate and can cause psychological harm. We all do this from time to time, but when we have suffered extreme trauma, we tend to engage in these patterns more often.

Aaron Beck and David Burns are experts in cognitive distortions. I used the top eleven distortions Beck and Burns list as most common. Writing things down and having them in front of me to reference works best, so I used the following list as my personal reference.

- All-or-Nothing Thinking/Polarized Thinking
- Overgeneralization
- Mental Filter
- Disqualifying the Positive
- Jumping to Conclusions—Mind Reading
- Jumping to Conclusions—Fortune Telling
- Magnification (Catastrophizing) or Minimization
- Emotional Reasoning
- Should Statements
- Labeling and Mislabeling
- Personalization

All-or-nothing thinking or polarized thinking is exactly what it sounds like. When we do this, we see things as black or white, one extreme or the other. For me, that was when I would tell myself, *I'm a failure. I can't do anything right.*

Overgeneralization is when we use a few experiences in our lives to make negative statements about ourselves. I would use the fact that I experienced bad relationships as proof that I was a failure in relationships.

A mental filter is when we also use an overgeneralization to filter our negative experiences and use that information to view ourselves or others as all bad. I would do this often in my relationships. If my partner did one bad thing, I catastrophized the whole relationship and labeled it as failing when in truth he was generally a good person. I could not focus on the good; instead, I saw only the bad.

Disqualifying the positive is the opposite of a mental filter. A person will refuse to accept positive input even when there is strong evidence to prove it. I often did that as a mom. I was so fixated on worrying that I was a bad mom that if someone told me I was a good mother, I refused to accept that. Even when they would list the things I did that proved I was a good mother, all I could see was where I had failed or fallen short.

Jumping to conclusions, mind reading, is when we believe we know what a person is thinking in a negative light. Boy was I guilty of that, and I still struggle with it. I easily fell into this distortion. After going through the false accusations and being investigated, I was super sensitive to people's facial expressions and I would jump to conclusions. If I saw people scowling, I immediately thought that they didn't like me or that they knew my secrets and were judging me.

Jumping to conclusions, fortune telling is very similar to the last. Those who do this jump to conclusions by making negative assumptions about what might happen in the future based on little to no evidence. I am guilty of that as well. Once I left the Marine Corps, I thought I had lost everything. Years passed, and I kept believing that I would never be successful at anything though I had no evidence to support that.

Magnification—catastrophizing—or minimization is when a person will magnify or minimize the importance of something negatively. At work I did my job extremely well, but I would find the slightest negative thing to focus on and use it to say that I wasn't good enough. If I received an award, I would minimize its importance by saying everyone else had gotten one too. I could not see myself as good, nor could I receive the praise I was often given.

Emotional reasoning is when we use our feelings as proof of something being true even when we know it's not a reasonable conclusion. Should statements are harmful and are another distortion that many people commonly believe or use on themselves and others. When I have done this, I have created false negative scenarios for myself that kept me from moving forward. The best example I have is when I kept saying to myself, *I should have known not to go with him to the beach.* These should statements made me feel guilty. They are extreme, and we never move past the pain to get to the truth when we hold onto these distortions.

Labeling and mislabeling occur when people label themselves or others in extreme negativity. Unfortunately, I did this often to myself as well. Since I had a few failed relationships, I labeled myself as stupid for having let that happen.

Personalization is just as it suggests—Some people will take everything as a personal attack on themselves or blame themselves for something without any evidence. It took me years to get over that one. I would blame myself when things didn't work out. I would blame myself when someone treated me badly. I took it personally when someone had a bad attitude and thought I caused their reaction or feelings.

Using these as my reference, I had to make a truthful look at my situation. In reality, there was no way I could have known for sure that going willingly with that male Marine would lead me to being sexually assaulted. Thinking I deserved that was a distorted belief, one I had to replace with a more realistic one. Hence, I reminded myself that I was not at fault and that there was no way for me to have known the outcome of that evening. I am not in control of how others behave or what they are capable of; there is no way for me to know what others are thinking and planning. I am responsible for only my actions and thoughts.

As easy as that may sound, it is not. This process needs to be repeated and often many times. Our minds are powerful especially when we have so many negative beliefs about ourselves that have become engrained. To get rid of such inaccurate beliefs, we have to tell ourselves the opposite of that belief repeatedly.

Taking Back Control

To find redemption in a traumatic experience, we need to learn about taking back our power. I felt I had little to no control. I had been taught that when I was a child. But this too is false. Taking back control does not mean you can control everything that happens to you either; it means you can learn to confidently move forward while embracing that sometimes you will not be in control but that you still can thrive.

We have to understand our values clearly if we want to stand firm in them. We may have inner conflict when we first introduce this thought change, but once we establish boundaries for ourselves and others, it becomes much easier. Taking back control of our thoughts and beliefs enables us to quiet those negative voices in our heads so we can take back control of our lives.

Acceptance

Being constantly reminded of your past can be exhausting. Once you come to a place of acceptance with what happened to you, the hurtful feelings associated with that memory will eventually diminish. Not that you should just accept every abusive or hurtful situation; instead, you should understand and accept that the event happened.

Often, I played in my head what had happened to me, repeatedly thinking of what I should have said or done differently, and that would drive me crazy and cause me anxiety and unnecessary stress. We all know we cannot change the past, so practicing acceptance of the memory and the event takes away its power and its hold on us. I was relieved once I mastered doing that. Now, I can discuss and tell others what happened without being bound to and smothered by the emotions previously attached to them. I can discuss them and sometimes feel the pain, but I can acknowledge them and let it go. The pain attached to the memory has diminished tremendously, and it no longer governs me.

11

REPORT

In the incertitude of battle, character matters. Every Marine fights with our Nation's expectation to represent it well at home and abroad. The values instilled not only direct every action, but unite every Marine, holding all Marines to the same high standard. —Marines.com

Other Tools for Healing

After years of just surviving, I acquired some other useful tools on the path to my healing. I work on myself every day. I believe I will always be a work in progress and it's ok. I think it helps to think this way. When you decide to give into the idea that you are a flawed individual just like everyone else, you will not program your mind to think you have to be perfect. The best way to be the best version of yourself is to continually work on enhancing what you have learned through experience—trial and error. This is a lifelong process too. I will share some of those tools so perhaps they can spark something in you if you need them and provide you with the beginning to your own path.

I will, however, suggest that you seek professional guidance if you feel that this is too difficult to do on your own. Having someone else provide you with insight and tools for enhancing YOU, will make your life a lot easier to maneuver in my opinion. Coming from the background I did, made it a lot more difficult for me to find my peace.

Learning to Be Present

After addressing my traumas and facing my truth, I realized there were other areas I needed to tackle and repair. It is important to re-learn or perhaps just learn to be present. Being present means you have learned to be cognizant and in the moment, so you are experiencing it fully. When you find that inner peace and can quiet the noise in your head, you can be present. I wondered how differently I would have dealt with adversity if anyone of significance had been present with me when I was a child and had made me feel valued and heard. My parents were not present the way I needed when I was a child. I don't necessarily blame them for that; they did the best they could with what they knew for the most part.

I grew up in an era when both parents had to work hard to provide for their families. Sometimes, that meant mine were overwhelmed and didn't have much left to give their children. We are not given manuals on how to parent, so most just repeat what they have experienced. I understand that things were difficult for them. Maneuvering through life's struggles, providing for the family, keeping a roof over our heads and a plate of food on the table while making sure we got a good education and didn't get caught up in drugs or gangs. It couldn't have been easy. Not to mention how children were supposed to be seen and not heard. Your parents told you to do something and you had better do it without question. Your feelings were not valued or considered; they were the parents, and they knew what was best for us.

I wanted to be a different parent. I always wanted my children to know that I valued their feelings. Being distant and emotionally detached was not how I wanted to parent. My children deserved a present parent. I wanted to be that for my children so badly. I know I wasn't always aware of this, and I lacked the ability to be there for my own children. As I got older, I learned this method and I practiced being present daily until it became natural for me.

I listen to who is speaking and give my full attention to them as best I can. I am not saying I am perfect at this because there are moments when I revert to my old patterns of behavior. The difference now is that I am aware of it and I work on being better the next time. Once you know better, you can do better.

Mindfulness

Mindfulness is a mental state achieved by focusing on the present. When you practice this, you will calmly acknowledge and accept your feelings, thoughts, and bodily sensations as valid. The important part of mindfulness is that you do not remain in these emotional states or feelings. You do not allow them to control you. Mindfulness is a technique that allows you to validate what you are feeling but then you work on moving past it.

It is important to do this because once you have moved past those feelings, it will help you avoid overreacting or becoming overwhelmed by what you are experiencing. This method of cognitive therapy works by allowing you to feel what you are feeling without judgment, so you don't obsess over your feelings. It brings awareness, compassion, and empathy into everything I do, so it limits the stress I experience.

Using this therapy helps me to be mindful of how joy and depression cannot share the same space. I have to intentionally choose which space I will purposefully reside in and walk in it. When I make this choice, I flourish. If I choose depression, I will walk in darkness. Ultimately, I walk in the path of happiness so I can walk in the glorious light I am intended to thrive in.

Mindfulness is also useful with everyday life. When you are mindful of how you are feeling, you can see how your actions sometimes are connected to how you are feeling that moment. Learn to have self-compassion so you are not too hard on yourself for the things you have done or said.

Awareness of others and how your actions can affect them is also important. Being mindful also allows you to be empathetic with others. Perhaps put yourself in what-if scenarios so you do not react harshly. For example, if someone cuts you off in traffic, instead of getting angry, you can ask yourself some what-ifs. What if that person was rushing to a hospital having found out that a loved one had just been admitted? Imaging this will calm your mind and give you compassion for their slighting you by cutting you off. Your anger can then be released, and you can move on without seeing them as an adversary.

You must focus your attentions on what works for you. Once you do, you can make adjustments and sometimes alter the path you are taking to fit your needs for that moment or situation. Just understand that what you choose will be unique to you just as the techniques I chose were for me. Also know that what works for you when you are twenty-five may not serve you when you're fifty. Remember, there are no one-size-fits-all treatments.

Ultimately, you have to come to terms with the trauma you survived, how you coped with it, and how you overcame obstacles along the way. You can appreciate how far you have come and where you are at this moment, and you can decide where you want to be.

Love Heals

As corny as it may sound, love does heal. Healing through love was the journey I chose. Thomas Wolfe wrote, "love is the ultimate expression of the will to live." I did not always love me, but I understood that in order to heal I needed to love myself first so that I could love others. Of course, I did not know initially that this was what I was doing. There was no way I could have told anyone that I loved myself. As a matter of fact, I hated myself. I felt like a failure on so many levels. I would look in the mirror and see someone who was worthless and unlovable. The reflection that stared back at me was one of an ugly individual on the inside and the outside. Sadly, that's all I saw. No one wanted me. How could anyone when I didn't even love myself? I was broken and damaged.

All of us should learn to just love through the pain. We can start with loving all aspects of ourselves good and bad alike. God made us who we are because He loves us all. If He can love us without conditions, through all of our ugliness and beauty, then why can't we love as well? When you figure out how to master that, it is easy to love yourself and others and attract the love you deserve. I wholeheartedly believe this because this was the path I took to find all the things I dreamed of, and I received them. I have experienced love as the catalyst that brought healing into fruition. I am not saying that love fixes every-thing; you have to do a lot of other work with self-love so you can get the wholeness you seek.

12

SAFETY

The greatest weapon in our arsenal is the fighting spirit found in each and every Marine. It's what enables Marines to get through tough times with an even tougher resilience. —Marines.com

Forgiveness

The concept of forgiveness was nothing I held onto nor did I want to give. After being betrayed, lied to, abused, and taken advantage of, I was bitter and angry. I was angry at myself because I thought I should have known better. I believed I had created the situations that led to what had happened to me.

I'd think, *Ok girl, if you were smarter or more aware, you wouldn't have placed yourself in the places or in the relationships doomed to lead you down a destructive path. Why would you go somewhere with a guy you barely knew without making sure you were safe? How could you trust someone you barely knew to give you a drink? You really suck Jeanette...if you would have reported what happened to you, that other girl could have been safe. It's all your fault!*

I was bitter because I wanted them all to pay. Forgiveness had no space in this equation. I envisioned all the ways I could make them suffer more than I had. Sometimes, I obsessed over those thoughts to the point that I would relive the betrayals, create different scenarios, and change the outcome so I seemed to be vindicated, but it was not real, so it would make me more anxious and even more angry at myself for not having taken the action I thought I should have at the time.

None of these feelings help. I promise you, the more you build up the hatred and bitterness you feel, the worse you will feel—mind, body, and soul. Anger and bitterness are cancers that eat at you from the inside until you are but a shell of your former self. How can you ever find love or love anyone when you are constantly holding onto past hurt and pain? How can anything good come into your life if you are obsessed with seeking retribution and inflicting hurt to others? Learn to let it go and live in the moment. Create new memories.

My redemption came when I forgave myself. The light came on in my head, and I realized that no matter what the circumstances, my horrible experiences were not the result of my actions. No one has the right to transgress or abuse you. I began to love myself once I forgave myself, but it takes time for that to happen as well. I had to do a lot of soul searching.

Helped by my therapist, Dr. Jimenez, I talked out the negative self-talk and used the tools she provided so I could retrain my brain with the new beliefs. I surrendered to my truth, and slowly, everything else came into place like pieces of a puzzle. Even some of the pieces I had lost eventually were found, and they found their rightful places.

At one time, I had a hard time just being in the same space with others. Panic and anxiety would take over, and I would want to run out of a room as soon as I walked in. In my mind, everyone in the room was whispering about me. They were staring at me thinking I was crazy, a bad person, or some other distorted belief that lingered in that moment in my head. My heart would race, my palms would become sweaty, and my head would start spinning. This whole time I was smiling, so no one knew these thoughts were going through my mind.

These episodes happened so often for me that I broke dates and promises to show up somewhere and did not attend events my friends or family invited me to. Even before I could attempt to muster the energy to make it to an event, I would make up all these scenarios in my head about how the interactions would play out. I would see myself walking into a room and notice that everyone was staring at me with contempt and disappointment in their eyes. I felt naked. I thought they could see all my secrets laid bare for all to scrutinize and make fun of. My heart would race, and I would become short of breath to the point that I felt I would pass out.

When people would invite me out, I would make up ridiculous excuses for why I couldn't go, and that disappointed them. Eventually, many friends just stopped inviting me anywhere. I became a flake. My family would gossip and make assumptions as to why I didn't show up here or there. They believed I thought I was better than them or was too busy doing things I was probably too embarrassed to tell them about. Most of them didn't even care enough to wonder why.

My anger and bitterness would rear their blackened heads, and I would beat myself up about my inability to just get it together and be normal. This vicious cycle happened so often. It was exhausting. I would get angry at my friends for inviting me, but then when they stopped inviting me to places or events, I would be angry at them for doing that. I would wallow in bitterness toward my family for their not understanding my struggle and making light of how I felt, but I barely shared anything with anyone fearing that they would think I was weak or crazy. So how could I expect anything different?

Now, instead of self-pity and angst regarding situations like these, I compromise with myself. First, I made a conscious decision to no longer just quickly agree to participate in occasions. I tell them to let me think about it or I will let them know later. Then, I give myself a time frame to respond to the invitation. I do a lot of self-talk too. I make deals with myself about which events I will attend. I ask myself, *Will this event take me out of my space peace and joy?* If it does not, I promise myself that once I commit, I will not back down unless there is a real situation I cannot avoid. I make a pact with myself that I will attend and be present at the event or occasion and enjoy it. I remind myself that if things get too overwhelming after an hour or so of being there and trying, I can gracefully excuse myself and leave.

This method works for me. Sometimes, I make it to the end of an event or special occasion, but other times, I don't. I no longer allow myself to be forced into situations where I am so uncomfortable that I become physically ill. So, I set boundaries or limits for myself as well. I push myself in healthy ways and engage in exposure therapy—a treatment developed to help individuals tackle their fears by exposing them to their fears and anxieties in a safe environment. Being blessed with a wonderful, caring, and loving husband makes my exposure therapy so much easier. Since I can tell him anything without him passing judgement, I can depend on him. If I suspect that a place or situation may trigger me, I let him know ahead of time so that he is aware in case I need moral support.

At times when I panicked at the thought of attending an event, I would find a safe person to help me through it. I would get excited about the possibility of attending a concert, for instance, but as the days got closer to the event, I would get panicky about being in a crowd. So, I would do some self-talk and convince myself that I could do this. I pushed myself into the scenario so that I could make it through and prove to myself that I was okay.

My husband made this easy for me. We would plan an outing, and if I felt anxiety creeping up, I would hold his hand. Just feeling him close to me and knowing he would never let anything, or anyone hurt me convinced me that I could make it through the event. I could let my guard down and be present in the experience. In the end, I would feel that I had conquered my fear and that I had an experience to reference when negative beliefs would creep into my heard. That process eventually made me stronger and less panicky.

13

DEPENDABILITY

"Amidst the stress and chaos of combat, there often is no telling how people will react. A hero one day may be a catatonic wreck the next. Some would say that's perfectly understandable. Marines say that's totally unacceptable. Marines demand dependability in all situations—on and off the battlefield. Leaders have consistency in crisis and do not over commit. They do what they say they'll do when they say they'll do it." Becoming A Marine Officer: The Ultimate Guide To Excelling At Officer Candidacy School, O.A. Pozhidaev,

p121

Find Healthy Structure in Your Environment

I was able to stay on the path to healing by finding healthy structures in my environment and sticking to it. We cannot control things that happen around us, but we can control the structures we create for our environments. Setting boundaries on who or what we allow into our space is pivotal to our mental well-being.

Being aware of negativity and removing it when I can, became my mantra. This even includes family members as some can be very toxic. Sometimes, this can become difficult, but being selfish about your mental health needs, should always be your priority.

When I was a child, I always gave in to others' needs and disregarded my own feelings. I was taught that my feelings and beliefs did not matter or did not take precedence. I also avoided making situations worse by speaking out. I'd rather help smooth things out or keep the peace. Retraining your mind to listen to that voice in your head when it warns you and follow your gut when it tells you something is wrong, is essential to walking this path. You can do those mental self-checks as I mentioned above, and when you find them true, remove yourself from the situation or space accordingly. Be assertive and stand your ground as well. You can do this in love without violating your values and disrupting your peace.

Find a Safe Place

I cannot remember a time when I felt completely safe growing up. Someone was always cursing, screaming, and yelling, a group would be fighting, or my space was being violated by strangers or outside family members taking precedence and strangers being moved into my family home to take over the space that should be sacred to me. Finding and keeping a safe place for my existence is essential for me to stay emotionally and mentally stable. Chaos and disruption cannot exist in peaceful and calming spaces as they are an oxymoron to our very existence

I created my safe place. My home is my safe place. I feel safe and at peace there. Anyone who disrupts that peace has to go, and that includes family. Protecting my peace means that I care for and safeguard my physical, emotional, mental, and spiritual self. Protecting my peace has become my personal goal on my path to healing. I decided it was in my own best interests to set boundaries for myself and others.

Oh, and just be aware, once you set boundaries, you will have individuals that will resist or say you are the bad one. Many people who have taken advantage of you in the past will back away and that may be a good thing. Fortunately, all the years I spent alone and in misery also taught me something else. I was no longer afraid to spend time alone. Actually, I enjoyed my time alone. So, I was no longer afraid to be alone if my boundaries required removing so many people that it left me alone for a while.

I used my time alone to write, draw, or do projects around the house. These can also be outlets of positivity. Use whatever is constructive and encouragingly effective for your well-being.

Have Strong Support

Being surrounded by a strong support system is vital to healing from trauma. If you don't have people who support you, you can easily fall back into old patterns of negative thoughts and beliefs. Having strong support is empowering. The support of friends and loved ones can make you more resilient in times of stress. In addition to shielding you from stress, having strong support can even help you recognize when you are struggling, and sometimes, those who support you may even notice it before you do. The stronger your support system, the better it is for your mental health recovery. Knowing that people have your back is vital to your healing. It fosters trust and security for you.

Having strong support also includes your friends and loved ones understanding that there will be times when we accept an invitation but flake and say we just don't want to go. When we do that, it just means we are maybe too tired to exert the energy to fake a smile, partake in small talk, or contribute in any social exchange.

Most of the time when I flake or say no, my body just has no energy to want to even try to do anything productive, talk to anyone or go anywhere. Those dealing with PTSD, trauma, or depression can be mentally fatigued to the point that it manifests in symptoms like body aches, nausea, headaches, and more. So when we say we don't feel good, that is often the case.

Strong support requires our loved ones to understand that it is exceptionally exhausting for us to just exist some days, so when we are present, please work on not overwhelming us with questions about how we feel, what we have been doing, or what we plan to do to get better. I promise you that when we get to the place of true healing, we will be more than willing to share those things freely. Until then, just be patient.

14

KNOWLEDGE

"The business of knowing what to do and how to do it lifts the leader above the crowd. Knowledge goes beyond the facts of the job; it is also knowledge of your team: who they are and what motivates them. It is knowledge of the culture in which you work, so that you understand what your superior's goals and missions are. And is also is self-knowledge: unflinchingly knowing your own strengths and weaknesses and having a desire to excel. Sharing knowledge with subordinates can feel to some leaders as though they are giving up control, and they may be loath to do so. In reality, though, leaders are not effective because they are the knowledge holders. Rather, the best leaders are the ones who make knowledge available to their teams and understand how best to deploy that knowledge in the best possible manner." Becoming A Marine Officer: The Ultimate Guide To Excelling At Officer Candidacy School, O.A. Pozhidaev, p124

For Loved Ones

As a family member, a friend, or a romantic partner of someone battling PTSD, you may be naturally inclined to want to do everything in your power to help fix things.

You're probably saying to yourself right now, *Isn't that what I'm supposed to do?*

Absolutely! But the way you approach a woman who has experienced military sexual trauma is not the same way as you approach a problem like a broken door or a clogged drain. You cannot magically fix it. There are no tools that can be used to fix us. You need to tread lightly. We are fragile, and if you push too much, that will make matters only worse. We will recoil and withdraw from everything and everyone. Sometimes, it is even more a disservice when you push too hard.

You know your loved one or friend, so use that knowledge to work with them. We know you want only what is best for us, but in the moment, we do not have the foresight to think that deeply. So, just find it in you to just be patient and love us gently – no judgement – no solutions – even no advice – just love.

As difficult as it may seem, for me, all I needed were these things.

Be an Emotional Support System

This support often encompasses verbal or nonverbal forms like physical comfort - hugs or holding hands (if we are emotionally capable of receiving it at that moment), affirmations of understanding, and listening and empathizing. Emotional support is where family and loved ones just listen to what you are struggling with and lovingly express empathy, love, trust, and caring. It may sound selfish of us to ask for this, but sometimes, this is all we can receive especially in the initial process of our healing.

When we are trying to overcome sexual trauma, some of us just need the reassurance that we are not alone with expressions of care and compassion from our loved ones

Just Listen

This support is easy. All we need sometimes is someone who will listen without judgment. Most don't realize that just holding someone's hand and honestly listening can be so helpful and therapeutic. We don't necessarily need our problems solved in that moment. Believe me, we will let you know when we need others' opinions or have a problem to be solved. Let us tell you what we need.

Just listen and allow us to vent and release all that toxic pain we hold inside. The act of us venting sometimes helps us lift off the weight we have been carrying.

Encourage, Don't Judge

Encouragement is also very important for us in the healing process. For the most part, we probably don't even know what we need, especially initially, but we always need encouragement. Let us know that you will always be there to support us unconditionally. You can encourage us without making us feel that you are judging our situation.

Please, oh please, never come to us with judgment. If we come to you with our struggles or concerns, the best thing you can do is just be supportive. If you don't have anything positive or helpful to say, don't say anything.

Respect Our Boundaries

Be mindful that women who have experienced sexual trauma have had their boundaries crossed on so many levels. Our boundaries are one of the only ways we have control. So, if we allow you into our circle of trust, please be mindful of not overstepping our boundaries. It is often difficult for us to express ourselves after surviving this trauma, so sometimes, you will need to err on the side of caution. Just give us our space, and don't be pushy.

There will be times when we will feel unsafe, so don't be offended if we need to sit in a corner with our backs against the wall just to feel some sense of security. It's not you. Control was taken away from us and needing to feel in control and safe go hand in hand. Crowds may sometimes heighten our sensitivity to intense feelings of being out of control. So, if we reach out and hold your hand, just tighten your grip as a small acknowledgement to be our security blanket for that moment. This worked for me often. Ultimately, you know your loved one the best, so take things in stride and just go with the flow without making us feel more overwhelmed than we already are.

Don't Treat Us as if We Are Broken

Looking at me as a fragile victim only made me angry. Having made it through and still being here not having given up shows just how strong we are. We are not what we've been through, so don't treat us as if we are broken.

One time, I met someone I thought I could trust, someone I felt safe with. I shared with him what had happened when I first got to Hawaii. I went all in and told him everything, even the fact that I couldn't remember specific details of that night. After I was done, I waited. Silence filled the room. I looked at his face and waited for something.

I wondered if he would say anything. I guess I was expecting him to have something deep to say that would make me feel better. Instead, he looked at me as if I were a bird with a broken wing, and I was mortified.

Please don't treat us as if we are broken; we already feel broken most of the time. We want people to treat us the same even though we know we are not the same. You might be able to distract us by making us laugh. When you treat us as if we are broken, all you're doing is proving to us that what we have been thinking all along about ourselves is right. We are survivors. We are not broken. We made it through the worst part, and now, we just need a hand every now and then as we continue our walk down the path of healing.

Don't Try to Fix Us

Most important, don't try to fix us. It's natural to hear the horrors of what we experienced and want to fix it for us. We are indeed dealing with painful and traumatic circumstances, but we are not broken. It may take us some time to find our way or even to want to get help, but once we do, let the professionals provide us the help we need. All I wanted from my family and friends was compassion, empathy, and unconditional love.

I recall a time when one of the guys I dated found out about my assault and harassment from one of my family members. Instead of taking that information so he could be helpful, he wanted to fix me. His idea of helping me was to tell me what I needed to do and how I could move past my fears by just getting over it. To add insult to injury, he believed that he was my salvation and that his purpose was to save the day by leading me to the solution.

The only person who can fix us is us.

Conclusion

Writing this book helped me on my path to healing and gave me a means to perhaps provide others with hope. I wrote this book from my perspective; it is all about how I perceived things throughout my life as they happened to me. There are instances of a few experiences of which I have no memory of, but I included them in this book using details given me by those closest to me at the time. Unfortunately, due to the trauma and/or possibly being drugged, I blocked some memories those experiences.

Never in this book have I intentionally enhanced or overstated any of my experiences. I truly tried to include my experiences as I remember them. I apologize in advance if anything offends or hurts anyone as that was certainly not my intention. I have written my experiences to the best of my ability, and on occasions or with conversations that I could not remember precisely, I have recreated them for readability. I always based my words on facts and what I experienced. Because we all perceive and experience situations differently, and that is part of life, others may have recalled things a little differently, and I honor and respect their truth as this is mine.

What I attempted in this book was to describe what it was like to experience but then survive military sexual trauma. I hope to provide some understanding of the mind of women who survived and live with PTSD daily so their family and loved ones can be more empathetic.

I have spent many years trying to figure out my life's path and how so many lives I have touched may have been damaged by my hurt. For my part, I am sorry. In my examination of my thoughts, memories, and feelings because of my own trauma, I determined there may be a component to my upbringing that had made me more susceptible to being sought out by my offenders. Often, we and our loved ones are doing the best we can with what we know, so we must learn to forgive them and ourselves. I have done this. I will not hold onto regret or anger toward those who hurt me because forgiveness releases me from the power they held over me.

I am so grateful for all the angels God placed in my path along the way to my healing. Whenever you are lost or needing something, God provides it. But it happens on His timeline. Perhaps that timeline includes His understanding what you need and when. It may also include the possibility of His knowing just the right time for you to be receptive to what He has for you.

For those who do not believe in God, He can be replaced with the universe. When I speak to my friends and family, I often use that phrase to encompass all possibilities so others may be more receptive to my message.

When you put out into the universe what you need, you will get it. When the universe is ready, it will give you what you need. Negative or positive, whatever you put out into the universe is always what you will receive. I received the help I needed in so many ways from people in my community, health care workers, mental health providers, television, books, etc.

I am grateful for Ayanla Vanzant of Ayanla Fix My Life; I faithfully watched her shows and learned so much from the healing paths she guided her guests on. I received her message loud and clear.

I thank Oprah Winfrey for her kind and calming words of enlightenment. I watched her shows throughout the years, and sometimes in my darkest moments, they kept me from going deeper into depression. Oprah provided me with the knowledge to seek peace and joy so my soul could learn to forgive the most important person of all—me. Oprah helped me discover that I could live a richer, more fulfilled life.

What I want for those who read this book to take away is that recovery after military sexual trauma is lifelong but possible. We are constantly striving to overcome our struggles, but it gets better. I found my path to redemption, and I continually walk it sometimes even pivoting and adjusting as I walk. I do not identify myself as a victim either; I am a survivor. Overcoming adversity has shown me just how strong I am. All the lies I was told beginning as a child until adulthood came from the pit of hell from individuals that were hurting as well. I know all the hurtful words they projected onto me were all lies.

I want those who have experienced military sexual trauma to know that we don't ever completely get over or move on from the trauma we've faced. After we give in to the fact that we have been through it, we have to make space in our lives for it, then we can learn to live with it and carry it. When I say "*carry it*" I mean use it to help others. I have transformed my tragedy into triumph and am a warrior for healing.

Stand tall, live in your truth, and let go of the guilt so you can thrive in spite of it. My dysfunctional upbringing, toxic familial relationships, and experience with military sexual trauma will not be my albatross; in fact these things have taught me to be stronger.

Now I have removed my camouflage of shame so that I can live authentically.

MY FAMILY

COMPLETE

About the Author

Jeanette is an Afro Latina born and raised in the Bronx, New York, to her Puerto Rican parents. Her father is a US Marine Corps Vietnam veteran, and after going to college for two years, she followed in his footsteps and joined the military. She enlisted and served during Desert Storm from 1991 to 1997. Jeanette was honorably discharged in 1997 as a sergeant and returned to civilian life with her two children.

She went back to school and earned a technical diploma in network engineering and data communications, an Associates' Degree in digital arts and animation, and a BA in multimedia arts and design. She completed this all while working on her trauma and mental health treatment and recovery.

Jeanette volunteered at the VA hospital in the Bronx and decided that she could do more by working directly in the system. She moved across the US from New York to Arizona and in 2010 worked for the Department of Veterans Affairs with the Vet Center—Readjustment Counseling Center. There, she utilized her multimedia art and administrative skills to help reach and assist her peers. As the office manager and outreach assistant at numerous veterans' conferences and events, she presented on benefits and provided resources for mental health and trauma and provided guidance for them on finding assistance for filing disability and compensation entitlements through the Veterans Administration.

Jeanette has always been a person striving to do more. In 2012, she accepted a job with the Veterans Administration as an executive administrative assistant to the chief nurse of the Southern Clinics in Cape

Coral, Florida. In 2014, she was promoted and accepted a job as the secretary to the deputy network director and the executive assistant to the chief nursing officer in Georgia. In 2016, she moved to Las Vegas to work with the Department of the Interior, as its administrative officer. She retired early in 2021 due to medical issues.

Jeanette lives in Texas with her soulmate, her husband Retired (USMC) Gunnery Sergeant and daughter. Their oldest son, Staff Sergeant Pizarro (USAF), lives in Las Vegas. Jeanette and her husband share two other daughters and a son—Brionna, a clinical social worker who lives in North Carolina, Demetria who lives in Utah with her biological mother, and Devon who also lives in Las Vegas.

Jeanette occasionally does freelance work as a multimedia artist designing websites and logos for small businesses creating corporate identity packages. She continues to help her veteran peers become successful and connect with their resources whenever she can. In 2021 she was the secretary and member of her local chapter NV-3 Sagebush Marines, Women Marines Association when they lived in Nevada. Jeanette also the media manager for and member of Colors of Lupus Nevada and Gamma Pi Rho Lupus Sorority, Inc.

JJ PIZARRO-HARPE

Resources for Those Needing Help with MST

Men Can Stop Rape: Creating Cultures Free From Violence is an organization "to mobilize men to use their strength for creating cultures free from violence, especially men's violence against women." https://mcsr.org/.

RAINN (Rape, Abuse, and Incest National Network) is the nation's largest anti-sexual violence organization. RAINN created and operates the National Sexual Assault Hotline (800–656–HOPE,online.rainn.org y rainn.org/es) in partnership with more than 1,000 sexual assault service providers across the country and operates the DoD Safe Helpline for the Department of Defense. RAINN also carries out programs to prevent sexual violence, help survivors, and ensure that perpetrators are brought to justice. https://www.rainn.org/.

Protect Our Defenders (POD) is the preeminent national human rights organization dedicated to ending sexual violence, victim retaliation, misogyny, sexual prejudice, and racism in the military and combating a culture that has allowed it to persist. https://www.protectourdefenders.com/about/.

Sexual Assault Prevention and Response Office (SAPRO) is the organization responsible for the oversight of Department of Defense (DoD) sexual assault policy. The DoD is committed to the prevention of sexual assault. The department has implemented a comprehensive policy to ensure the safety, dignity, and well-being of all members of the armed forces. Our men and women serving throughout the world deserve nothing less, and their leaders —both military and civilian—are committed to maintaining a workplace environment that rejects sexual assault and reinforces prevention, response and accountability. https://www.sapr.mil/.

Safe Helpline is the Department of Defense's (DoD) sole hotline for members of the DoD community affected by sexual assault. Safe Helpline is a completely anonymous, confidential, specialized service providing help and information 24/7. A Safe Helpline user can access one-on-one support, peer-to-peer support, information, resources, and self-care exercises to aid in their recovery. Since 2011, Safe Helpline has provided support and resources to thousands of members of the DoD community. SAFE Helpline: 877–995–5247. www.Safe-helpline.org.

VA Medical Center Downloadable Fact Sheets and Tools. https://www.mental-health.va.gov/msthome/resources.asp.
Commander, Navy Installation Command Notification: Sexual Assault Resources. https://www.cnic.navy.mil/ffr/family_readiness/fleet_and_family_support_program/sexual_assault_prevention_and_response/resources.html.

Disabled American Veterans Military Sexual Trauma Resources. https://www.dav.org/veterans/resources/military-sexual-trauma-mst/.

National Sexual Violence Resource Center (NSVRC): Military Sexual Trauma Resource List. https://www.nsvrc.org/blogs/military-sexual-trauma-resource-list.

Vet Centers are community-based counseling centers that provide a wide range of social and psychological services including professional readjustment counseling to eligible veterans and active-duty service members including National Guard and Reserve components and their families. Readjustment counseling is offered to make a successful transition from military to civilian life or after a traumatic event experienced in the military. Individual, group, marriage, and family counseling are offered in addition to referral and connection to other VA or community benefits and services. Vet Center counselors and outreach staff, many of whom are veterans, are experienced and prepared to discuss the tragedies of war, loss, grief, and transition after trauma. https://www.vetcenter.va.gov/index.asp.

DoD Safe Helpline. Sexual assault can be reported at any time regardless of the amount of time since the assault. Early reporting provides the best opportunity to gather testimony from possible witnesses before their memories fade or they move to other locations. DoD Safe Helpline provides confidential crisis intervention, support, and information to service members of the DoD community who have been sexually assaulted. DoD Safe Helpline is available 24/7 worldwide at 877–995–5247.
Other resources are the local medical treatment facility; Military Police/Criminal

Investigation Division; your commander, supervisor, or first sergeant; the chaplain, social services, family advocacy, and legal services. Army psychiatric counselors and chaplains are confidential counseling channels. You can also call the National Sexual Assault Hotline, which is free and confidential 24/7 at 800-656-HOPE.

Jeanette is an Afro Latina born and raised in the Bronx, New York, to her Puerto Rican parents, Carlos and Anna. Her father is a US Marine Corps Vietnam veteran, and after going to college for two years, she followed in his footsteps and joined the Marine Corps. She enlisted and served during Desert Storm from 1991 to 1997. Jeanette was honorably discharged in 1997 as a sergeant and returned to civilian life with her two children, Darren and Devon.

She went back to school and earned a technical diploma in network engineering and data communications, an associates' degree in digital arts and animation, and a BA in multimedia arts and design. She completed this all while working on her trauma and mental health treatment and recovery.

Jeanette volunteered at the VA hospital in the Bronx and decided that she could do more by working directly in the system. She moved across the US from New York to Arizona and in 2010 worked for the Department of Veterans Affairs with the Vet Center—Readjustment Counseling Center. There, she utilized her multimedia art and administrative skills to help reach and assist her peers. As the office manager and outreach assistant at numerous veterans' conferences and events, she presented on benefits and provided resources for mental health and trauma and provided guidance for them on finding assistance for filing disability and compensation entitlements through the Veterans Administration. Jeanette has always been a person striving to do more. In 2012, she accepted a job with the Veterans Administration as an executive administrative assistant to the chief nurse of the Southern Clinics in Cape Coral, Florida. In 2014, she was promoted and accepted a job as the secretary to the deputy network director of VISN 7 and the executive assistant to the chief nursing officer in Georgia. In 2016, she moved to Las Vegas to work with the Department of the Interior, US Fish and Wildlife Office as its administrative officer. She retired early in 2021 due to medical issues.

Jeanette lives in Las Vegas with her soulmate, her husband Retired (USMC) Gunnery Sergeant Darius Harpe and daughter Erica. Her oldest son, Staff Sergeant (USAF) Darren Pizarro, also lives in Las Vegas. Darius and Jeanette share two other daughters and a son—Brionna, a clinical social worker who lives in North Carolina, Demetria, who lives in Utah with her biological mother, and son Devon, who lives in Las Vegas.

Jeanette occasionally does freelance work as a multimedia artist designing websites and logos for small businesses creating corporate

identity packages. She continues to help her veteran peers become successful and connect with their resources whenever she can.
She is a member of her local chapter NV-3 Sagebush Marines, Women Marines Association. Jeanette is the media and marketing representative for and member of Colors of Lupus Nevada and Gamma Pi Rho Lupus Sorority.